"Wisdom, according to the book of Proverbs, is a skill in the art of godly living. It is the application of the truth of the Word of God to every aspect of one's life. I love Proverbs and find myself going back to it almost daily. Any growth in wisdom is ultimately a growth in the fear of and love for the Lord. What could be better than this?"

—Josh Patterson
Lead Pastor, Ministry Leadership—The Village Church

"The choices we make in our lives determine our character and ultimately our destiny. This is why we need God's wisdom, and this is why I love the book of Proverbs. If you desire to live a life that honors the Lord, there is no greater place to start than this book."

—Jarret Stephens
Teaching Pastor, Prestonwood Baptist Church

"The famous preacher Charles Spurgeon once said: 'He that would be wise, let him read the Proverbs.' If you would be wise then drink from this devotional on Proverbs. You will find it to be 'a fountain of wisdom' and 'a tree of life' for you and your family."

—Dr. Justin W. Bass
Lead Pastor, 1042 Church

"Wisdom is an oft misunderstood and neglected aspect of modern life. In a world consumed with sound-bites, frivolity, and selfies, people are in desperate need of wisdom. In this helpful guide, my friend Trog, leads us on a journey toward true wisdom—that which is found in Christ—wisdom that aids us in both living lives pleasing to God but also in effectively serving the world as redemptive interpreters of reality. I recommend this book to you as a helpful tool in obtaining that which God describes as being 'more precious than rubies.'"

—S. Michael Craven
Author, *Uncompromised Faith: Overcoming Our Culturalized Christianity* and
Founder of Battle for Truth

"Life's journey is filled with complex choices that require God's wisdom. Trog's thirty-one-day challenge will assure that you will be wise and not a fool."

—Mark Penick, PhD

"Many males are growing up without the presence and teaching of a father in their home. Want to be a better husband, father, and friend? Read and apply Proverbs to your life. It will help you grow into a man that possesses godly wisdom, Christian character, personal integrity, and practical understanding of what is right and fair."

—Jeff Scruggs
Co-founder of Hope Matters Marriage Ministries, Inc. and
Author, *I Do Again*

"I have found the book of Proverbs to be the single most influential guide for my life. Through *A Walk to Wisdom*, Trog has created an outstanding resource. One that is certain to inspire all who read it as they capture the most precious wisdom of the ages that is certain to impact lives!"

—Ray Sanders
CEO, Water4

"What a great resource to have the book of Proverbs in such an accessible form! Proverbs is a practical yet powerful source of daily wisdom for every aspect of life, including relationships, business and parenting. Soak it in."

—Stan Dobbs
Founder of Apartment Life Ministries

"Trog's compilation of the Proverbs is a gem that allows the reader to engage the timeless truths of wisdom in an easy-to-follow, practical, and transformative way. Simply a must-have, go-to book for those that want to be wise."

—Duffy Johnson
M.Div. Missions Pastor, Highland Park Presbyterian Church,
Dallas, TX

"When I finally decided to get serious about my relationship with Christ and Trog began discipling me, the first thing he recommended was reading a Proverb a day. In a culture that has doubts about the relevance of the Bible, one just has to look to the Proverbs to see that the wisdom of God absolutely stands today and will continue to stand forever."

—J.T. Patton
Lead Pastor, Freshwater Church, Springfield, MO

"At no other time have we been bombarded with so many messages and so much information that can either help us or hinder us. The book of Proverbs remains a solid source of wisdom that helps us as individuals, families, and followers of Christ seeking to fight injustice, love each other, and not make as many foolish decisions in life."

—Andy Robinson
Founder and President of Fifty-Eight Foundation

"Trog Trogdon is a man who is walking wisely and changing Dallas for God's glory. I'm thankful that he is challenging us, through this new resource, to read just one Proverb a day. *A Walk to Wisdom* is a profound and helpful challenge to seek and cry out for understanding from God."

—Dave Sterrett
Author, *Why Trust Jesus*? and Co-author, *I Am Second*

"I love the book of Proverbs. Growing up, my mom would always be sure that I had taken my vitamin in the morning: One-a-Day. The book of Proverbs is like that. In this edition, the reader can take in every one of the 915 verses in the book of Proverbs in its thirty-one manageable chapters. One-a-Day. Simple. But the wisdom and truth that comes along with a careful, steady reading of Proverbs will bring comfort, character, and strength. This is a great gift to us who want God's extreme wisdom for our time. I plan to use it . . . and give many copies away."

—The Very Rev. David H. Roseberry
Dean/Rector, Christ Church (Anglican), Plano, TX

"The wisdom and guiding principles that come from the book of Proverbs are so important to obtaining success in life that Proverbs is the first entire book in all of Scripture that I read to my three children. Our world is filled with more knowledge and college degrees than at any other time in history, but people are more confused than ever because the world is deficient of men and women grounded in godly wisdom. If you want to discover more of God's will and increase in wisdom, this resource on the book of Proverbs is an excellent place to start."

—Dr. Jon Lineberger
Assistant Vice President, Dallas Baptist University and
Author, *What God Did With A Mess Like Me*

"The book of Proverbs is all about getting on a path and living a life of wisdom. Whether you want to learn about managing money, relationships, or your mouth, this is a must read."

—Justen Quebe
Lubbock Campus Pastor, Harvest Christian Fellowship

"Years ago, prior to entering full-time vocational ministry, I looked in vain for this very tool Trog has produced. I wanted something, in addition to my Bible that I could lay on my desk specifically focused on Proverbs and wisdom. Now I have it. God generously gives us wisdom if we'll just ask and pursue Him. I am excited that the Lord used Trog to produce this simple, yet profound tool to expose us daily to God's infinite wisdom."

—Mike Congrove
Executive Director, Empower Sudan

"Simply put . . . what Trog has put his efforts toward is wanted, needed, and should become a handbook for Church discipleship of all ages. Memorizing these Scriptures from an early age will help secure our children on the narrow road that is becoming narrower and narrower everyday. As a pastor's wife for over forty years, I have looked to no avail for something just like this for our congregations. Thank you, Trog, for your faithfulness to the Kingdom."

—Leesa Bellesi
Partnering Founder, Kingdom Assignment Trilogy
www.GoServeSomeone.org

"A Walk to Wisdom is a refreshing journey through the book of Proverbs. It asks thought-provoking questions and has helped me to experience the Scriptures in a new way. It is a great tool for anyone seeking wisdom and a deeper understanding of the book of Proverbs."

—Josh Havens
Lead Singer, The Afters

A Walk to Wisdom

A Walk to Wisdom

31 Days Through the Proverbs

Trog Trogdon

A Walk to Wisdom

Brown Christian Press
16250 Knoll Trail Drive
Suite 205
Dallas, Texas 75248
www.BrownChristianPress.com
(972) 381-0009

A New Era in Publishing®

Names: Trogdon, Trog, author.
Title: A walk to wisdom : 31 days through the Proverbs / Trog Trogdon.
Description: Dallas, Texas : Brown Christian Press, [2014]
Identifiers: ISBN 9781612541808
Subjects: LCSH: Bible. Proverbs--Commentaries. | Wisdom--Biblical teaching. | Christian life.
Classification: LCC BS1465.53 .T76 2014 | DDC 223/.707--dc23

ISBN 978-1-61254-180-8
LCCN 2014947185

Printed in the United States
10 9 8 7 6 5 4 3

For more information or to contact the author, please go to www.AWalkToWisdom.com or send an e-mail to trogtrogdon@gmail.com.

This book is dedicated to Mike Fechner, my mentor, my friend, my brother in Christ, and hero in the faith of whom "the world was not worthy." I love and miss you, Mike, and am forever grateful for your wisdom, counsel, and faithful witness of seeking first the Kingdom over the years. My life and ministry would not be the same without your incredible influence in my life.

Contents

Foreword

Wisdom is what every person wants, especially those that fear God. The Lord puts in the hearts of all His disciples a desire to live life from His perspective. Indeed a heart of wisdom is ever growing, as a follower of Jesus seeks to know Him and understand His Word. Wisdom hunting is a process of humble learning that lasts a lifetime. The wise never arrive in their acquisition of God's knowledge, wisdom, and principles for living. Students continually seek wisdom.

When I was thirty-one years old, an older friend described to me his wisdom journey. I listened intently because his life was worth emulating. He was the kind of man you wanted to be like, the spiritual leader of his family, a respected businessman, and a student of the Scriptures. Astonishingly for ten years, he read a chapter daily in Proverbs based on the day of the month. For example, on May third, he read the third chapter of Proverbs and meditated on its meaning for his life. I quickly understood what made him such a good role model. It was the wisdom he gathered and applied from the Word of God, specifically the book of Proverbs.

I felt the Holy Spirit prompting me to accept that same challenge; so from age thirty-one to age forty-one, I read a chapter in Proverbs daily based on the day of the month. It was uncanny how what I was learning mirrored my life experiences. Everything I read—from the wise management of money to avoiding sexual temptation—began to transform my behavior. Ideas about parenting, marriage, and relationships started to strongly motivate my selfless service to others.

The other very real reality of practicing the principles of Proverbs is—it works. If we humbly and consistently follow these extremely practical teachings, we grow in Christ's character and in our knowledge of Him. Once the Holy Spirit illuminates our minds to understand the enormous benefit of behaving according to the Lord's principles, then we are responsible for embedding them into our daily walk. Knowledge without application only contributes to pseudo spirituality that lacks life. Proverbs applied produces faith fruit.

I am so thrilled God has called Trog to compile this very practical book on God's wisdom. The pages in this compact book of writings will change your life for the better. Do you want to be a leader worth following? A father who is admired or a mother who is appreciated? What about a child who is pleasant? Or a disciple of Jesus who is growing in grace? Are you looking to love the Lord and people with authentic actions? If so, then seek to know God's heart on how to live life, which He beautifully lays out in the principles of Proverbs.

Proverbs is not a magic wand that works out everything we encounter in life, but it is a guide to go with our prayers and experiences. Like a porter who carries the equipment of his men up a mountain climb, follow Jesus as He reveals His ways in these wise and ancient words that have proven true for over three thousand years. Wisdom has a track record of trust in God, love for God, and fear of God. So by God's grace, be wise!

A fellow servant of Jesus,
Boyd Bailey, Roswell, GA
Founder of WisdomHunters.com

Acknowledgments

To my wife, who makes every ministry effort possible and exemplifies the Proverbs 31 wife whose "lamp does not go out at night." Thank you sweetheart for loving and following me along this journey of faith in Christ.

To Aaron Helms, one of my best college friends, who first told me about "The Proverbs Challenge" and his father Marlon Helms who started the legacy of this book years ago.

To my dad, Duane Trogdon, who made this project possible and raised me in the way of wisdom.

To my mom, Jane Parsons, for her never-ending love and support.

To J.T. Patton, who has encouraged and sharpened me daily in my walk with Christ over the past seven to eight years of life.

To Dr. Justin Bass, who gave me my first pastoral position as an elder at 1042 Church and always answers my theological questions with wonderful, biblical insight.

To Daris Lee, who not only listens to wise counsel but shares it with those around him.

To Willie "Right" Charles, who is full of wisdom and walks the obedient life of discipleship.

To Bonton and the whole "family," who has accepted me as one of their own.

To Milli Brown and her outstanding group of professionals at Brown Books Publishing Group.

Introduction

I currently serve as an Urban Gardener and missionary in a neighborhood in south Dallas that has had a very rough reputation over the past few decades. The needs in the community are numerous, but the Kingdom of God is breaking through as the Spirit of the Lord is transforming hearts and minds. It's exciting to be a part of the progress. As I began serving in this capacity and talking with different residents, the main burden on my heart was the great lack of fatherly wisdom in the neighborhood. There seemed to be so many bad choices being made and terrible repercussions as a result of those choices, that it broke my heart. Many of these bad decisions, I believe, would have been different if they had had access to the wise counsel and sound advice of a loving and God-fearing father. As I began to ponder this, I couldn't think of a better way to get this fatherly wisdom into the hands of my friends and "family" than to produce a single book of Proverbs that they could carry around and frequently reference. After all, the purpose of Proverbs is "*To know wisdom and instruction, to understand words of insight, to receive instruction in wise dealing, in righteousness, justice, and equity; to give prudence to the simple, knowledge and discretion to the youth.*" *(Proverbs 1:2–4)*

This book of Proverbs, that is so full of fatherly wisdom, has to be my favorite book in the entire Bible! Years ago, when I was a senior in college and a freshman in the faith, a dear friend of mine named Aaron Helms told me about the "Proverbs Challenge" for the first time. He gave me simple and straightforward advice that has stuck with me ever since. He said, "There are thirty-one days in an average month and there are thirty-one chapters in the book of Proverbs. Just open your Bible each day and read the chapter in Proverbs that corresponds with each date. After a year, you will have read through the whole book about a dozen times." Being an uncomplicated man and one that didn't like to read all that much at the time, this was just the kind of advice that I needed. It was easy to learn and hard to forget!

Since that time, I have read Proverbs more than any other book in the Bible. I can't say that I've read it a dozen times a year, but I can say that in all of my Bibles it seems to be the most marked up, highlighted and underlined portion of the text. I even printed out a copy of Proverbs and keep it with me in my planner. I've read, studied, and shared the wisdom found in Proverbs with many people and groups over the years, and I find myself applying it on a daily basis. The wisdom that I've found in this book has helped me in almost every aspect of my life; in marriage, parenting, business, ministry, finances, relationships, and more. It's hard to convey the impact that this book has had on me and it is my prayer that it will change the course of your life and the lives of your loved ones forever as well.

As Proverbs 3:13–15 says, "*Blessed is the one who finds wisdom, and the one who gets understanding, for the gain from her is better than gain from silver and her profit better than gold. She is more precious than jewels, and nothing you desire can compare with her.*"

How to Use This Book

The Bible can be an intimidating book, especially if you are new to the faith or have never read it before. It's not just one book but really sixty-six books wrapped into a single volume with a total of 1,189 chapters and roughly 31,103 verses. This can easily seem like a daunting task to tackle for the natural eye and that is partly why this book, *A Walk to Wisdom*, has been compiled. It allows you to take a big (seemingly overwhelming) book and break it down into bite-sized pieces that are easy to read, reference, and, most importantly, apply to your life. We've all heard the saying, "you have to eat an elephant one bite at a time." It is my great desire that this compilation will give you a bite-sized option to get into God's Word on a daily basis and in turn, transform your mind and life.

Use This Book as

A Journal: This is not a normal book for you to read and then put away to be forever forgotten. This book is designed for you to "read, mark, learn, and inwardly digest" as the great prayer of our faith states. The layout has purposefully been set up for you to interact with the text—to highlight, underline, and reflect upon the content, capturing thoughts at every turn. Each chapter of Proverbs has a corresponding place for you to take notes, and at the end of each chapter, there are reflection questions designed to help you think through, remember, and apply what the Lord teaches you along the way.

A Daily Devotional: There are thirty-one chapters in the book of Proverbs. If you can remember what day of the month it is, then you can remember what chapter in this book you are supposed to read; it's that simple. For example, if it is March 17th, then you would read Proverbs chapter seventeen. I challenge you (and myself) to read through this book twelve times each year.

A Foundational Book for Your Faith: I believe Proverbs is a foundational book for your faith because it is easy to read and understand the meaning and purpose of each passage. As you begin to grow in wisdom and knowledge through the content of this one book, you will begin to see how other portions of Scripture fit perfectly together. It's amazing how many verses in Proverbs come to mind as I study other books of the Bible!

It is a great foundation to build a biblical knowledge-base upon and it will help you grow strong in your faith.

A Legacy: At its core, this is a legacy book. One that you will read, reread, and hopefully pass down to your kids and grandkids, blessing them with your journey of faith, in written form, for years to come. I can't think of a greater gift to give to your children than a marked-up and highlighted book of the Bible with your thoughts and heart inscribed onto each page.

A Witnessing Tool: This book will clearly present the gospel message. Get copies to give away. Study it with your friends that are on the fringe of our faith. Start a small group at your church and invite non-members and non-believers. Everybody wants and needs wisdom: from teachers to politicians, businessmen to baseball players. Let this desire for wisdom be your opportunity to get them the gospel message!

As you work your way through this book, you will notice that it is not full of commentary or typical devotional material. This is done on purpose. It is the word of God that is *"living and active, sharper than any two-edged sword, piercing to the division of soul and of spirit, of joints and of marrow, and discerning the thoughts and intentions of the heart" (Hebrews 4:12)*. So instead of giving you my thoughts and opinions throughout, the goal is to allow the Word of God to work in your heart and mind and let the Holy Spirit guide you into all truth as you read and think about the words on each page. One of my favorite prayers to pray before reading God's word is Psalm 119:18 which states, *"Open my eyes, that I may behold wondrous things out of your law."* I invite you to pray this prayer each time you sit down to read the day's Proverb and just watch what the Lord does. Get ready for an exciting journey!

Blessed Lord, who caused all holy Scriptures to be written for our learning: Grant us so to hear them, read, mark, learn, and inwardly digest them, that we may embrace and ever hold fast the blessed hope of everlasting life, which you have given us in our Savior Jesus Christ; who lives and reigns with you and the Holy Spirit, one God, for ever and ever. Amen.

—Book of Common Prayer, pg. 236

Proverbs

The fear of the Lord is the beginning of wisdom,
and the knowledge of the Holy One is insight.

Proverbs 9:10

Day 1

Proverbs 1

The Beginning of Knowledge

1 The proverbs of Solomon, son of David, king of Israel:

2 To know wisdom and instruction, to understand words of insight,

3 to receive instruction in wise dealing, in righteousness, justice, and equity;

4 to give prudence to the simple, knowledge and discretion to the youth—

5 Let the wise hear and increase in learning, and the one who understands obtain guidance,

6 to understand a proverb and a saying, the words of the wise and their riddles.

7 The fear of the Lord is the beginning of knowledge; fools despise wisdom and instruction.

The Enticement of Sinners

8 Hear, my son, your father's instruction, and forsake not your mother's teaching,

9 for they are a graceful garland for your head and pendants for your neck.

10 My son, if sinners entice you, do not consent.

11 If they say, "Come with us, let us lie in wait for blood; let us ambush the innocent without reason;

12 like Sheol let us swallow them alive, and whole, like those who go down to the pit;

13 we shall find all precious goods, we shall fill our houses with plunder;

14 throw in your lot among us; we will all have one purse"—

15 my son, do not walk in the way with them; hold back your foot from their paths,

16 for their feet run to evil, and they make haste to shed blood.

17 For in vain is a net spread in the sight of any bird,

18 but these men lie in wait for their own blood; they set an ambush for their own lives.

19 Such are the ways of everyone who is greedy for unjust gain; it takes away the life of its possessors.

The Call of Wisdom

20 Wisdom cries aloud in the street, in the markets she raises her voice;

21 at the head of the noisy streets she cries out; at the entrance of the city gates she speaks:

22 "How long, O simple ones, will you love being simple? How long will scoffers delight in their scoffing and fools hate knowledge?

23 If you turn at my reproof,[a] behold, I will pour out my spirit to you; I will make my words known to you.

24 Because I have called and you refused to listen, have stretched out my hand and no one has heeded,

25 because you have ignored all my counsel and would have none of my reproof,

26 I also will laugh at your calamity; I will mock when terror strikes you,

27 when terror strikes you like a storm and your calamity comes like a whirlwind, when distress and anguish come upon you.

28 Then they will call upon me, but I will not answer; they will seek me diligently but will not find me.

29 Because they hated knowledge and did not choose the fear of the Lord,

30 would have none of my counsel and despised all my reproof,

31 therefore they shall eat the fruit of their way, and have their fill of their own devices.

32 For the simple are killed by their turning away, and the complacency of fools destroys them;

33 but whoever listens to me will dwell secure and will be at ease, without dread of disaster."

---

a. Proverbs 1:23 Or *Will you turn away at my reproof?*

Notes...

Reflection Questions...

As you read today's chapter in Proverbs

1. Did a verse or group of verses catch your attention? If so, why?

   a. How can you apply this wisdom in your life today/this week?

   b. Will you make the effort to commit this verse (or verses) to memory?

2. Did you see a recurring theme?

   a. If so, why is this theme important in our lives?

   b. How could applying this wisdom change your life and/or your relationships with others?

3. Did you find something you could praise God for? Take a moment to thank Him for a few blessings today.

4. Did you find a verse that you can incorporate in your time of prayer with God?

5. Were you reminded of any mistakes that you've made in the past? Take a moment and ask the Lord to forgive you and give you the strength to walk in His ways moving forward.

Day 2

Proverbs 2

The Value of Wisdom

1 My son, if you receive my words and treasure up my commandments with you,

2 making your ear attentive to wisdom and inclining your heart to understanding;

3 yes, if you call out for insight and raise your voice for understanding,

4 if you seek it like silver and search for it as for hidden treasures,

5 then you will understand the fear of the Lord and find the knowledge of God.

6 For the Lord gives wisdom; from his mouth come knowledge and understanding;

7 he stores up sound wisdom for the upright; he is a shield to those who walk in integrity,

8 guarding the paths of justice and watching over the way of his saints.

9 Then you will understand righteousness and justice and equity, every good path;

10 for wisdom will come into your heart, and knowledge will be pleasant to your soul;

11 discretion will watch over you, understanding will guard you,

12 delivering you from the way of evil, from men of perverted speech,

13 who forsake the paths of uprightness to walk in the ways of darkness,

14 who rejoice in doing evil and delight in the perverseness of evil,

15 men whose paths are crooked, and who are devious in their ways.

16 So you will be delivered from the forbidden[a] woman, from the adulteress[b] with her smooth words,

17 who forsakes the companion of her youth and forgets the covenant of her God;

18 for her house sinks down to death, and her paths to the departed;[c]

19 none who go to her come back, nor do they regain the paths of life.

20 So you will walk in the way of the good and keep to the paths of the righteous.

21 For the upright will inhabit the land, and those with integrity will remain in it,

22 but the wicked will be cut off from the land, and the treacherous will be rooted out of it.

---

a. Proverbs 2:16 Hebrew *strange* | b. Proverbs 2:16 Hebrew *foreign woman* | c. Proverbs 2:18 Hebrew *to the Rephaim*

Notes...

Reflection Questions...

As you read today's chapter in Proverbs

1. Did a verse or group of verses catch your attention? If so, why?

   a. How can you apply this wisdom in your life today/this week?

   b. Will you make the effort to commit this verse (or verses) to memory?

2. Did you see a recurring theme?

   a. If so, why is this theme important in our lives?

   b. How could applying this wisdom change your life and/or your relationships with others?

3. Did you find something you could praise God for? Take a moment to thank Him for a few blessings today.

4. Did you find a verse that you can incorporate in your time of prayer with God?

5. Were you reminded of any mistakes that you've made in the past? Take a moment and ask the Lord to forgive you and give you the strength to walk in His ways moving forward.

Day 3

Proverbs 3

Trust in the Lord with All Your Heart

1 My son, do not forget my teaching, but let your heart keep my commandments,

2 for length of days and years of life and peace they will add to you.

3 Let not steadfast love and faithfulness forsake you; bind them around your neck; write them on the tablet of your heart.

4 So you will find favor and good success[a] in the sight of God and man.

5 Trust in the Lord with all your heart, and do not lean on your own understanding.

6 In all your ways acknowledge him, and he will make straight your paths.

7 Be not wise in your own eyes; fear the Lord, and turn away from evil.

8 It will be healing to your flesh[b] and refreshment[c] to your bones.

9 Honor the Lord with your wealth and with the firstfruits of all your produce;

10 then your barns will be filled with plenty, and your vats will be bursting with wine.

11 My son, do not despise the Lord's discipline or be weary of his reproof,

12 for the Lord reproves him whom he loves, as a father the son in whom he delights.

Blessed Is the One Who Finds Wisdom

13 Blessed is the one who finds wisdom, and the one who gets understanding,

14 for the gain from her is better than gain from silver and her profit better than gold.

15 She is more precious than jewels, and nothing you desire can compare with her.

16 Long life is in her right hand; in her left hand are riches and honor.

17 Her ways are ways of pleasantness, and all her paths are peace.

18 She is a tree of life to those who lay hold of her; those who hold her fast are called blessed.

19 The Lord by wisdom founded the earth; by understanding he established the heavens;

20 by his knowledge the deeps broke open, and the clouds drop down the dew.

21 My son, do not lose sight of these—keep sound wisdom and discretion,

22 and they will be life for your soul and adornment for your neck.

23 Then you will walk on your way securely, and your foot will not stumble.

24 If you lie down, you will not be afraid; when you lie down, your sleep will be sweet.

25 Do not be afraid of sudden terror or of the ruin[d] of the wicked, when it comes,

26 for the Lord will be your confidence and will keep your foot from being caught.

27 Do not withhold good from those to whom it is due,[e] when it is in your power to do it.

28 Do not say to your neighbor, "Go, and come again, tomorrow I will give it"—when you have it with you.

29 Do not plan evil against your neighbor, who dwells trustingly beside you.

30 Do not contend with a man for no reason, when he has done you no harm.

31 Do not envy a man of violence and do not choose any of his ways,

32 for the devious person is an abomination to the Lord, but the upright are in his confidence.

33 The Lord's curse is on the house of the wicked, but he blesses the dwelling of the righteous.

34 Toward the scorners he is scornful, but to the humble he gives favor.[f]

35 The wise will inherit honor, but fools get[g] disgrace.

---

a. Proverbs 3:4 Or *repute* | b. Proverbs 3:8 Hebrew *navel* | c. Proverbs 3:8 Or *medicine* | d. Proverbs 3:25 Hebrew *storm* | e. Proverbs 3:27 Hebrew *Do not withhold good from its owners* | f. Proverbs 3:34 Or *grace* | g. Proverbs 3:35 The meaning of the Hebrew word is uncertain

Notes...

Reflection Questions...

As you read today's chapter in Proverbs

1. Did a verse or group of verses catch your attention? If so, why?

   ____

   ____

   a. How can you apply this wisdom in your life today/this week?

   ____

   ____

   b. Will you make the effort to commit this verse (or verses) to memory?

   ____

   ____

2. Did you see a recurring theme?

   ____

   ____

   a. If so, why is this theme important in our lives?

   ____

   ____

   b. How could applying this wisdom change your life and/or your relationships with others?

   ____

   ____

3. Did you find something you could praise God for? Take a moment to thank Him for a few blessings today.

   ____

   ____

4. Did you find a verse that you can incorporate in your time of prayer with God?

   ____

   ____

5. Were you reminded of any mistakes that you've made in the past? Take a moment and ask the Lord to forgive you and give you the strength to walk in His ways moving forward.

   ____

   ____

Day 4

Proverbs 4

A Father's Wise Instruction

1 Hear, O sons, a father's instruction, and be attentive, that you may gain[a] insight,

2 for I give you good precepts; do not forsake my teaching.

3 When I was a son with my father, tender, the only one in the sight of my mother,

4 he taught me and said to me, "Let your heart hold fast my words; keep my commandments, and live.

5 Get wisdom; get insight; do not forget, and do not turn away from the words of my mouth.

6 Do not forsake her, and she will keep you; love her, and she will guard you.

7 The beginning of wisdom is this: Get wisdom, and whatever you get, get insight.

8 Prize her highly, and she will exalt you; she will honor you if you embrace her.

9 She will place on your head a graceful garland; she will bestow on you a beautiful crown."

10 Hear, my son, and accept my words, that the years of your life may be many.

11 I have taught you the way of wisdom; I have led you in the paths of uprightness.

12 When you walk, your step will not be hampered, and if you run, you will not stumble.

13 Keep hold of instruction; do not let go; guard her, for she is your life.

14 Do not enter the path of the wicked, and do not walk in the way of the evil.

15 Avoid it; do not go on it; turn away from it and pass on.

16 For they cannot sleep unless they have done wrong; they are robbed of sleep unless they have made someone stumble.

17 For they eat the bread of wickedness and drink the wine of violence.

18 But the path of the righteous is like the light of dawn, which shines brighter and brighter until full day.

19 The way of the wicked is like deep darkness; they do not know over what they stumble.

20 My son, be attentive to my words; incline your ear to my sayings.

21 Let them not escape from your sight; keep them within your heart.

22 For they are life to those who find them, and healing to all their[b] flesh.

23 Keep your heart with all vigilance, for from it flow the springs of life.

24 Put away from you crooked speech, and put devious talk far from you.

25 Let your eyes look directly forward, and your gaze be straight before you.

26 Ponder[c] the path of your feet; then all your ways will be sure.

27 Do not swerve to the right or to the left; turn your foot away from evil.

---

a. Proverbs 4:1 Hebrew *know* | b. Proverbs 4:22 Hebrew *his* | c. Proverbs 4:26 Or *Make level*

Notes...

Reflection Questions...

As you read today's chapter in Proverbs

1. Did a verse or group of verses catch your attention? If so, why?

    a. How can you apply this wisdom in your life today/this week?

    b. Will you make the effort to commit this verse (or verses) to memory?

2. Did you see a recurring theme?

    a. If so, why is this theme important in our lives?

    b. How could applying this wisdom change your life and/or your relationships with others?

3. Did you find something you could praise God for? Take a moment to thank Him for a few blessings today.

4. Did you find a verse that you can incorporate in your time of prayer with God?

5. Were you reminded of any mistakes that you've made in the past? Take a moment and ask the Lord to forgive you and give you the strength to walk in His ways moving forward.

Day 5

Proverbs 5

Warning Against Adultery

1 My son, be attentive to my wisdom; incline your ear to my understanding,

2 that you may keep discretion, and your lips may guard knowledge.

3 For the lips of a forbidden[a] woman drip honey, and her speech[b] is smoother than oil,

4 but in the end she is bitter as wormwood, sharp as a two-edged sword.

5 Her feet go down to death; her steps follow the path to[c] Sheol;

6 she does not ponder the path of life; her ways wander, and she does not know it.

7 And now, O sons, listen to me, and do not depart from the words of my mouth.

8 Keep your way far from her, and do not go near the door of her house,

9 lest you give your honor to others and your years to the merciless,

10 lest strangers take their fill of your strength, and your labors go to the house of a foreigner,

11 and at the end of your life you groan, when your flesh and body are consumed,

12 and you say, "How I hated discipline, and my heart despised reproof!

13 I did not listen to the voice of my teachers or incline my ear to my instructors.

14 I am at the brink of utter ruin in the assembled congregation."

15 Drink water from your own cistern, flowing water from your own well.

16 Should your springs be scattered abroad, streams of water in the streets?

17 Let them be for yourself alone, and not for strangers with you.

18 Let your fountain be blessed, and rejoice in the wife of your youth,

19 a lovely deer, a graceful doe. Let her breasts fill you at all times with delight; be intoxicated[d] always in her love.

20 Why should you be intoxicated, my son, with a forbidden woman and embrace the bosom of an adulteress?[e]

21 For a man's ways are before the eyes of the Lord, and he ponders[f] all his paths.

22 The iniquities of the wicked ensnare him, and he is held fast in the cords of his sin.

23 He dies for lack of discipline, and because of his great folly he is led astray.

---

a. Proverbs 5:3 Hebrew *strange*; also verse 20 | b. Proverbs 5:3 Hebrew *palate* | c. Proverbs 5:5 Hebrew *lay hold of* | d. Proverbs 5:19 Hebrew *be led astray*; also verse 20 | e. Proverbs 5:20 Hebrew *a foreign woman* | f. Proverbs 5:21 Or *makes level*

Notes...

Reflection Questions...

As you read today's chapter in Proverbs

1. Did a verse or group of verses catch your attention? If so, why?

    ____

    ____

    a. How can you apply this wisdom in your life today/this week?

    ____

    ____

    b. Will you make the effort to commit this verse (or verses) to memory?

    ____

    ____

2. Did you see a recurring theme?

    ____

    ____

    a. If so, why is this theme important in our lives?

    ____

    ____

    b. How could applying this wisdom change your life and/or your relationships with others?

    ____

    ____

3. Did you find something you could praise God for? Take a moment to thank Him for a few blessings today.

    ____

    ____

4. Did you find a verse that you can incorporate in your time of prayer with God?

    ____

    ____

5. Were you reminded of any mistakes that you've made in the past? Take a moment and ask the Lord to forgive you and give you the strength to walk in His ways moving forward.

    ____

    ____

Day 6

Proverbs 6

Practical Warnings

1 My son, if you have put up security for your neighbor, have given your pledge for a stranger,

2 if you are snared in the words of your mouth, caught in the words of your mouth,

3 then do this, my son, and save yourself, for you have come into the hand of your neighbor: go, hasten,[a] and plead urgently with your neighbor.

4 Give your eyes no sleep and your eyelids no slumber;

5 save yourself like a gazelle from the hand of the hunter,[b] like a bird from the hand of the fowler.

6 Go to the ant, O sluggard; consider her ways, and be wise.

7 Without having any chief, officer, or ruler,

8 she prepares her bread in summer and gathers her food in harvest.

9 How long will you lie there, O sluggard? When will you arise from your sleep?

10 A little sleep, a little slumber, a little folding of the hands to rest,

11 and poverty will come upon you like a robber, and want like an armed man.

12 A worthless person, a wicked man, goes about with crooked speech,

13 winks with his eyes, signals[c] with his feet, points with his finger,

14 with perverted heart devises evil, continually sowing discord;

15 therefore calamity will come upon him suddenly; in a moment he will be broken beyond healing.

16 There are six things that the Lord hates, seven that are an abomination to him:

17 haughty eyes, a lying tongue, and hands that shed innocent blood,

18 a heart that devises wicked plans, feet that make haste to run to evil,

19 a false witness who breathes out lies, and one who sows discord among brothers.

Warnings Against Adultery

20 My son, keep your father's commandment, and forsake not your mother's teaching.

21 Bind them on your heart always; tie them around your neck.

22 When you walk, they[d] will lead you; when you lie down, they will watch over you; and when you awake, they will talk with you.

23 For the commandment is a lamp and the teaching a light, and the reproofs of discipline are the way of life,

24 to preserve you from the evil woman,[e] from the smooth tongue of the adulteress.[f]

25 Do not desire her beauty in your heart, and do not let her capture you with her eyelashes;

26 for the price of a prostitute is only a loaf of bread,[g] but a married woman[h] hunts down a precious life.

27 Can a man carry fire next to his chest and his clothes not be burned?

28 Or can one walk on hot coals and his feet not be scorched?

29 So is he who goes in to his neighbor's wife; none who touches her will go unpunished.

30 People do not despise a thief if he steals to satisfy his appetite when he is hungry,

31 but if he is caught, he will pay sevenfold; he will give all the goods of his house.

32 He who commits adultery lacks sense; he who does it destroys himself.

33 He will get wounds and dishonor, and his disgrace will not be wiped away.

34 For jealousy makes a man furious, and he will not spare when he takes revenge.

35 He will accept no compensation; he will refuse though you multiply gifts.

---

a. Proverbs 6:3 Or *humble yourself* | b. Proverbs 6:5 Hebrew lacks *of the hunter* | c. Proverbs 6:13 Hebrew *scrapes* | d. Proverbs 6:22 Hebrew *it*; three times in this verse | e. Proverbs 6:24 Revocalization (compare Septuagint) yields *from the wife of a neighbor* | f. Proverbs 6:24 Hebrew *the foreign woman* | g. Proverbs 6:26 Or (compare Septuagint, Syriac, Vulgate) *for a prostitute leaves a man with nothing but a loaf of bread* | h. Proverbs 6:26 Hebrew *a man's wife*

Notes...

Reflection Questions...

As you read today's chapter in Proverbs

1. Did a verse or group of verses catch your attention? If so, why?

   a. How can you apply this wisdom in your life today/this week?

   b. Will you make the effort to commit this verse (or verses) to memory?

2. Did you see a recurring theme?

   a. If so, why is this theme important in our lives?

   b. How could applying this wisdom change your life and/or your relationships with others?

3. Did you find something you could praise God for? Take a moment to thank Him for a few blessings today.

4. Did you find a verse that you can incorporate in your time of prayer with God?

5. Were you reminded of any mistakes that you've made in the past? Take a moment and ask the Lord to forgive you and give you the strength to walk in His ways moving forward.

Day 7

Proverbs 7

Warning Against the Adulteress

1 My son, keep my words and treasure up my commandments with you;

2 keep my commandments and live; keep my teaching as the apple of your eye;

3 bind them on your fingers; write them on the tablet of your heart.

4 Say to wisdom, "You are my sister," and call insight your intimate friend,

5 to keep you from the forbidden[a] woman, from the adulteress[b] with her smooth words.

6 For at the window of my house I have looked out through my lattice,

7 and I have seen among the simple, I have perceived among the youths, a young man lacking sense,

8 passing along the street near her corner, taking the road to her house

9 in the twilight, in the evening, at the time of night and darkness.

10 And behold, the woman meets him, dressed as a prostitute, wily of heart.[c]

11 She is loud and wayward; her feet do not stay at home;

12 now in the street, now in the market, and at every corner she lies in wait.

13 She seizes him and kisses him, and with bold face she says to him,

14 "I had to offer sacrifices,[d] and today I have paid my vows;

15 so now I have come out to meet you, to seek you eagerly, and I have found you.

16 I have spread my couch with coverings, colored linens from Egyptian linen;

17 I have perfumed my bed with myrrh, aloes, and cinnamon.

18 Come, let us take our fill of love till morning; let us delight ourselves with love.

19 For my husband is not at home; he has gone on a long journey;

20 he took a bag of money with him; at full moon he will come home."

21 With much seductive speech she persuades him; with her smooth talk she compels him.

22 All at once he follows her, as an ox goes to the slaughter, or as a stag is caught fast[e]

23 till an arrow pierces its liver; as a bird rushes into a snare; he does not know that it will cost him his life.

24 And now, O sons, listen to me, and be attentive to the words of my mouth.

25 Let not your heart turn aside to her ways; do not stray into her paths,

26 for many a victim has she laid low, and all her slain are a mighty throng.

27 Her house is the way to Sheol, going down to the chambers of death.

---

a. Proverbs 7:5 Hebrew *strange* | b. Proverbs 7:5 Hebrew *the foreign woman* | c. Proverbs 7:10 Hebrew *guarded in heart* | d. Proverbs 7:14 Hebrew *peace offerings* | e. Proverbs 7:22 Probable reading (compare Septuagint, Vulgate, Syriac); Hebrew *as an anklet for the discipline of a fool*

Notes...

Reflection Questions...

As you read today's chapter in Proverbs

1. Did a verse or group of verses catch your attention? If so, why?

    a. How can you apply this wisdom in your life today/this week?

    b. Will you make the effort to commit this verse (or verses) to memory?

2. Did you see a recurring theme?

    a. If so, why is this theme important in our lives?

    b. How could applying this wisdom change your life and/or your relationships with others?

3. Did you find something you could praise God for? Take a moment to thank Him for a few blessings today.

4. Did you find a verse that you can incorporate in your time of prayer with God?

5. Were you reminded of any mistakes that you've made in the past? Take a moment and ask the Lord to forgive you and give you the strength to walk in His ways moving forward.

Day 8

Proverbs 8

The Blessings of Wisdom

1 Does not wisdom call? Does not understanding raise her voice?

2 On the heights beside the way, at the crossroads she takes her stand;

3 beside the gates in front of the town, at the entrance of the portals she cries aloud:

4 "To you, O men, I call, and my cry is to the children of man.

5 O simple ones, learn prudence; O fools, learn sense.

6 Hear, for I will speak noble things, and from my lips will come what is right,

7 for my mouth will utter truth; wickedness is an abomination to my lips.

8 All the words of my mouth are righteous; there is nothing twisted or crooked in them.

9 They are all straight to him who understands, and right to those who find knowledge.

10 Take my instruction instead of silver, and knowledge rather than choice gold,

11 for wisdom is better than jewels, and all that you may desire cannot compare with her.

12 "I, wisdom, dwell with prudence, and I find knowledge and discretion.

13 The fear of the LORD is hatred of evil. Pride and arrogance and the way of evil and perverted speech I hate.

14 I have counsel and sound wisdom; I have insight; I have strength.

15 By me kings reign, and rulers decree what is just;

16 by me princes rule, and nobles, all who govern justly.[a]

17 I love those who love me, and those who seek me diligently find me.

18 Riches and honor are with me, enduring wealth and righteousness.

19 My fruit is better than gold, even fine gold, and my yield than choice silver.

20 I walk in the way of righteousness, in the paths of justice,

21 granting an inheritance to those who love me, and filling their treasuries.

22 "The Lord possessed[b] me at the beginning of his work,[c] the first of his acts of old.

23 Ages ago I was set up, at the first, before the beginning of the earth.

24 When there were no depths I was brought forth, when there were no springs abounding with water.

25 Before the mountains had been shaped, before the hills, I was brought forth,

26 before he had made the earth with its fields, or the first of the dust of the world.

27 When he established the heavens, I was there; when he drew a circle on the face of the deep,

28 when he made firm the skies above, when he established[d] the fountains of the deep,

29 when he assigned to the sea its limit, so that the waters might not transgress his command, when he marked out the foundations of the earth,

30 then I was beside him, like a master workman, and I was daily his[e] delight, rejoicing before him always,

31 rejoicing in his inhabited world and delighting in the children of man.

32 "And now, O sons, listen to me: blessed are those who keep my ways.

33 Hear instruction and be wise, and do not neglect it.

34 Blessed is the one who listens to me, watching daily at my gates, waiting beside my doors.

35 For whoever finds me finds life and obtains favor from the Lord,

36 but he who fails to find me injures himself; all who hate me love death."

---

a. Proverbs 8:16 Most Hebrew manuscripts; many Hebrew manuscripts, Septuagint *govern the earth* | b. Proverbs 8:22 Or *fathered*; Septuagint *created* | c. Proverbs 8:22 Hebrew *way* | d. Proverbs 8:28 The meaning of the Hebrew is uncertain | e. Proverbs 8:30 Or *daily filled with*

Notes...

Reflection Questions...

As you read today's chapter in Proverbs

1. Did a verse or group of verses catch your attention? If so, why?

    a. How can you apply this wisdom in your life today/this week?

    b. Will you make the effort to commit this verse (or verses) to memory?

2. Did you see a recurring theme?

    a. If so, why is this theme important in our lives?

    b. How could applying this wisdom change your life and/or your relationships with others?

3. Did you find something you could praise God for? Take a moment to thank Him for a few blessings today.

4. Did you find a verse that you can incorporate in your time of prayer with God?

5. Were you reminded of any mistakes that you've made in the past? Take a moment and ask the Lord to forgive you and give you the strength to walk in His ways moving forward.

Day 9

Proverbs 9

The Way of Wisdom

1 Wisdom has built her house; she has hewn her seven pillars.

2 She has slaughtered her beasts; she has mixed her wine; she has also set her table.

3 She has sent out her young women to call from the highest places in the town,

4 "Whoever is simple, let him turn in here!" To him who lacks sense she says,

5 "Come, eat of my bread and drink of the wine I have mixed.

6 Leave your simple ways,[a] and live, and walk in the way of insight."

7 Whoever corrects a scoffer gets himself abuse, and he who reproves a wicked man incurs injury.

8 Do not reprove a scoffer, or he will hate you; reprove a wise man, and he will love you.

9 Give instruction[b] to a wise man, and he will be still wiser; teach a righteous man, and he will increase in learning.

10 The fear of the Lord is the beginning of wisdom, and the knowledge of the Holy One is insight.

11 For by me your days will be multiplied, and years will be added to your life.

12 If you are wise, you are wise for yourself; if you scoff, you alone will bear it.

The Way of Folly

13 The woman Folly is loud; she is seductive[c] and knows nothing.

14 She sits at the door of her house; she takes a seat on the highest places of the town,

15 calling to those who pass by, who are going straight on their way,

16 "Whoever is simple, let him turn in here!" And to him who lacks sense she says,

17 "Stolen water is sweet, and bread eaten in secret is pleasant."

18 But he does not know that the dead[d] are there, that her guests are in
the depths of Sheol.

---

a. Proverbs 9:6 Or *Leave the company of the simple* | b. Proverbs 9:9 Hebrew lacks *instruction* | c. Proverbs 9:13 Or *full of simpleness* | d. Proverbs 9:18 Hebrew *Rephaim*

Notes...

Reflection Questions...

As you read today's chapter in Proverbs

1. Did a verse or group of verses catch your attention? If so, why?

    a. How can you apply this wisdom in your life today/this week?

    b. Will you make the effort to commit this verse (or verses) to memory?

2. Did you see a recurring theme?

    a. If so, why is this theme important in our lives?

    b. How could applying this wisdom change your life and/or your relationships with others?

3. Did you find something you could praise God for? Take a moment to thank Him for a few blessings today.

4. Did you find a verse that you can incorporate in your time of prayer with God?

5. Were you reminded of any mistakes that you've made in the past? Take a moment and ask the Lord to forgive you and give you the strength to walk in His ways moving forward.

Day 10
Proverbs 10

The Proverbs of Solomon

1 The proverbs of Solomon. A wise son makes a glad father, but a foolish son is a sorrow to his mother.

2 Treasures gained by wickedness do not profit, but righteousness delivers from death.

3 The Lord does not let the righteous go hungry, but he thwarts the craving of the wicked.

4 A slack hand causes poverty, but the hand of the diligent makes rich.

5 He who gathers in summer is a prudent son, but he who sleeps in harvest is a son who brings shame.

6 Blessings are on the head of the righteous, but the mouth of the wicked conceals violence.

7 The memory of the righteous is a blessing, but the name of the wicked will rot.

8 The wise of heart will receive commandments, but a babbling fool will come to ruin.

9 Whoever walks in integrity walks securely, but he who makes his ways crooked will be found out.

10 Whoever winks the eye causes trouble, and a babbling fool will come to ruin.

11 The mouth of the righteous is a fountain of life, but the mouth of the wicked conceals violence.

12 Hatred stirs up strife, but love covers all offenses.

13 On the lips of him who has understanding, wisdom is found, but a rod is for the back of him who lacks sense.

14 The wise lay up knowledge, but the mouth of a fool brings ruin near.

15 A rich man's wealth is his strong city; the poverty of the poor is their ruin.

16 The wage of the righteous leads to life, the gain of the wicked to sin.

17 Whoever heeds instruction is on the path to life, but he who rejects reproof leads others astray.

18 The one who conceals hatred has lying lips, and whoever utters slander is a fool.

19 When words are many, transgression is not lacking, but whoever restrains his lips is prudent.

20 The tongue of the righteous is choice silver; the heart of the wicked is of little worth.

21 The lips of the righteous feed many, but fools die for lack of sense.

22 The blessing of the Lord makes rich, and he adds no sorrow with it.[a]

23 Doing wrong is like a joke to a fool, but wisdom is pleasure to a man of understanding.

24 What the wicked dreads will come upon him, but the desire of the righteous will be granted.

25 When the tempest passes, the wicked is no more, but the righteous is established forever.

26 Like vinegar to the teeth and smoke to the eyes, so is the sluggard to those who send him.

27 The fear of the Lord prolongs life, but the years of the wicked will be short.

28 The hope of the righteous brings joy, but the expectation of the wicked will perish.

29 The way of the Lord is a stronghold to the blameless, but destruction to evildoers.

30 The righteous will never be removed, but the wicked will not dwell in the land.

31 The mouth of the righteous brings forth wisdom, but the perverse tongue will be cut off.

32 The lips of the righteous know what is acceptable, but the mouth of the wicked, what is perverse.

---

a. Proverbs 10:22 Or *and toil adds nothing to it*

Notes...

Reflection Questions...

As you read today's chapter in Proverbs

1. Did a verse or group of verses catch your attention? If so, why?

   a. How can you apply this wisdom in your life today/this week?

   b. Will you make the effort to commit this verse (or verses) to memory?

2. Did you see a recurring theme?

   a. If so, why is this theme important in our lives?

   b. How could applying this wisdom change your life and/or your relationships with others?

3. Did you find something you could praise God for? Take a moment to thank Him for a few blessings today.

4. Did you find a verse that you can incorporate in your time of prayer with God?

5. Were you reminded of any mistakes that you've made in the past? Take a moment and ask the Lord to forgive you and give you the strength to walk in His ways moving forward.

Day 11

Proverbs 11

1 A false balance is an abomination to the Lord, but a just weight is his delight.

2 When pride comes, then comes disgrace, but with the humble is wisdom.

3 The integrity of the upright guides them, but the crookedness of the treacherous destroys them.

4 Riches do not profit in the day of wrath, but righteousness delivers from death.

5 The righteousness of the blameless keeps his way straight, but the wicked falls by his own wickedness.

6 The righteousness of the upright delivers them, but the treacherous are taken captive by their lust.

7 When the wicked dies, his hope will perish, and the expectation of wealth[a] perishes too.

8 The righteous is delivered from trouble, and the wicked walks into it instead.

9 With his mouth the godless man would destroy his neighbor, but by knowledge the righteous are delivered.

10 When it goes well with the righteous, the city rejoices, and when the wicked perish there are shouts of gladness.

11 By the blessing of the upright a city is exalted, but by the mouth of the wicked it is overthrown.

12 Whoever belittles his neighbor lacks sense, but a man of understanding remains silent.

13 Whoever goes about slandering reveals secrets, but he who is trustworthy in spirit keeps a thing covered.

14 Where there is no guidance, a people falls, but in an abundance of counselors there is safety.

15 Whoever puts up security for a stranger will surely suffer harm, but he who hates striking hands in pledge is secure.

16 A gracious woman gets honor, and violent men get riches.

17 A man who is kind benefits himself, but a cruel man hurts himself.

18 The wicked earns deceptive wages, but one who sows righteousness gets a sure reward.

19 Whoever is steadfast in righteousness will live, but he who pursues evil will die.

20 Those of crooked heart are an abomination to the Lord, but those of blameless ways are his delight.

21 Be assured, an evil person will not go unpunished, but the offspring of the righteous will be delivered.

22 Like a gold ring in a pig's snout is a beautiful woman without discretion.

23 The desire of the righteous ends only in good; the expectation of the wicked in wrath.

24 One gives freely, yet grows all the richer; another withholds what he should give, and only suffers want.

25 Whoever brings blessing will be enriched, and one who waters will himself be watered.

26 The people curse him who holds back grain, but a blessing is on the head of him who sells it.

27 Whoever diligently seeks good seeks favor,[b] but evil comes to him who searches for it.

28 Whoever trusts in his riches will fall, but the righteous will flourish like a green leaf.

29 Whoever troubles his own household will inherit the wind, and the fool will be servant to the wise of heart.

30 The fruit of the righteous is a tree of life, and whoever captures souls is wise.

31 If the righteous is repaid on earth, how much more the wicked and the sinner!

---

a. Proverbs 11:7 Or *of his strength*, or *of iniquity* | b. Proverbs 11:27 Or *acceptance*

Notes...

Reflection Questions...

As you read today's chapter in Proverbs

1. Did a verse or group of verses catch your attention? If so, why?

    a. How can you apply this wisdom in your life today/this week?

    b. Will you make the effort to commit this verse (or verses) to memory?

2. Did you see a recurring theme?

    a. If so, why is this theme important in our lives?

    b. How could applying this wisdom change your life and/or your relationships with others?

3. Did you find something you could praise God for? Take a moment to thank Him for a few blessings today.

4. Did you find a verse that you can incorporate in your time of prayer with God?

5. Were you reminded of any mistakes that you've made in the past? Take a moment and ask the Lord to forgive you and give you the strength to walk in His ways moving forward.

Day 12

Proverbs 12

1 Whoever loves discipline loves knowledge, but he who hates reproof is stupid.

2 A good man obtains favor from the Lord, but a man of evil devices he condemns.

3 No one is established by wickedness, but the root of the righteous will never be moved.

4 An excellent wife is the crown of her husband, but she who brings shame is like rottenness in his bones.

5 The thoughts of the righteous are just; the counsels of the wicked are deceitful.

6 The words of the wicked lie in wait for blood, but the mouth of the upright delivers them.

7 The wicked are overthrown and are no more, but the house of the righteous will stand.

8 A man is commended according to his good sense, but one of twisted mind is despised.

9 Better to be lowly and have a servant than to play the great man and lack bread.

10 Whoever is righteous has regard for the life of his beast, but the mercy of the wicked is cruel.

11 Whoever works his land will have plenty of bread, but he who follows worthless pursuits lacks sense.

12 Whoever is wicked covets the spoil of evildoers, but the root of the righteous bears fruit.

13 An evil man is ensnared by the transgression of his lips, but the righteous escapes from trouble.

14 From the fruit of his mouth a man is satisfied with good, and the work of a man's hand comes back to him.

15 The way of a fool is right in his own eyes, but a wise man listens to advice.

16 The vexation of a fool is known at once, but the prudent ignores an insult.

17 Whoever speaks[a] the truth gives honest evidence, but a false witness utters deceit.

18 There is one whose rash words are like sword thrusts, but the tongue of the wise brings healing.

19 Truthful lips endure forever, but a lying tongue is but for a moment.

20 Deceit is in the heart of those who devise evil, but those who plan peace have joy.

21 No ill befalls the righteous, but the wicked are filled with trouble.

22 Lying lips are an abomination to the Lord, but those who act faithfully are his delight.

23 A prudent man conceals knowledge, but the heart of fools proclaims folly.

24 The hand of the diligent will rule, while the slothful will be put to forced labor.

25 Anxiety in a man's heart weighs him down, but a good word makes him glad.

26 One who is righteous is a guide to his neighbor,[b] but the way of the wicked leads them astray.

27 Whoever is slothful will not roast his game, but the diligent man will get precious wealth.[c]

28 In the path of righteousness is life, and in its pathway there is no death.

---

a. Proverbs 12:17 Hebrew *breathes out* | b. Proverbs 12:26 Or *The righteous chooses his friends carefully* | c. Proverbs 12:27 Or *but diligence is precious wealth*

Notes...

Reflection Questions...

As you read today's chapter in Proverbs

1. Did a verse or group of verses catch your attention? If so, why?

    a. How can you apply this wisdom in your life today/this week?

    b. Will you make the effort to commit this verse (or verses) to memory?

2. Did you see a recurring theme?

    a. If so, why is this theme important in our lives?

    b. How could applying this wisdom change your life and/or your relationships with others?

3. Did you find something you could praise God for? Take a moment to thank Him for a few blessings today.

4. Did you find a verse that you can incorporate in your time of prayer with God?

5. Were you reminded of any mistakes that you've made in the past? Take a moment and ask the Lord to forgive you and give you the strength to walk in His ways moving forward.

Day 13
Proverbs 13

1 A wise son hears his father's instruction, but a scoffer does not listen to rebuke.

2 From the fruit of his mouth a man eats what is good, but the desire of the treacherous is for violence.

3 Whoever guards his mouth preserves his life; he who opens wide his lips comes to ruin.

4 The soul of the sluggard craves and gets nothing, while the soul of the diligent is richly supplied.

5 The righteous hates falsehood, but the wicked brings shame[a] and disgrace.

6 Righteousness guards him whose way is blameless, but sin overthrows the wicked.

7 One pretends to be rich, yet has nothing; another pretends to be poor, yet has great wealth.

8 The ransom of a man's life is his wealth, but a poor man hears no threat.

9 The light of the righteous rejoices, but the lamp of the wicked will be put out.

10 By insolence comes nothing but strife, but with those who take advice is wisdom.

11 Wealth gained hastily[b] will dwindle, but whoever gathers little by little will increase it.

12 Hope deferred makes the heart sick, but a desire fulfilled is a tree of life.

13 Whoever despises the word brings destruction on himself, but he who reveres the commandment will be rewarded.

14 The teaching of the wise is a fountain of life, that one may turn away from the snares of death.

15 Good sense wins favor, but the way of the treacherous is their ruin.[c]

16 In everything the prudent acts with knowledge, but a fool flaunts his folly.

17 A wicked messenger falls into trouble, but a faithful envoy brings healing.

18 Poverty and disgrace come to him who ignores instruction, but whoever heeds reproof is honored.

19 A desire fulfilled is sweet to the soul, but to turn away from evil is an abomination to fools.

20 Whoever walks with the wise becomes wise, but the companion of fools will suffer harm.

21 Disaster[d] pursues sinners, but the righteous are rewarded with good.

22 A good man leaves an inheritance to his children's children, but the sinner's wealth is laid up for the righteous.

23 The fallow ground of the poor would yield much food, but it is swept away through injustice.

24 Whoever spares the rod hates his son, but he who loves him is diligent to discipline him.[e]

25 The righteous has enough to satisfy his appetite, but the belly of the wicked suffers want.

---

a. Proverbs 13:5 Or *stench* | b. Proverbs 13:11 Or *by fraud* | c. Proverbs 13:15 Probable reading (compare Septuagint, Syriac, Vulgate); Hebrew *is rugged*, or *is an enduring rut* | d. Proverbs 13:21 Or *Evil* | e. Proverbs 13:24 Or *who loves him disciplines him early*

Notes...

Reflection Questions...

As you read today's chapter in Proverbs

1. Did a verse or group of verses catch your attention? If so, why?

   a. How can you apply this wisdom in your life today/this week?

   b. Will you make the effort to commit this verse (or verses) to memory?

2. Did you see a recurring theme?

   a. If so, why is this theme important in our lives?

   b. How could applying this wisdom change your life and/or your relationships with others?

3. Did you find something you could praise God for? Take a moment to thank Him for a few blessings today.

4. Did you find a verse that you can incorporate in your time of prayer with God?

5. Were you reminded of any mistakes that you've made in the past? Take a moment and ask the Lord to forgive you and give you the strength to walk in His ways moving forward.

Day 14

Proverbs 14

1 The wisest of women builds her house, but folly with her own hands tears it down.

2 Whoever walks in uprightness fears the Lord, but he who is devious in his ways despises him.

3 By the mouth of a fool comes a rod for his back,[a] but the lips of the wise will preserve them.

4 Where there are no oxen, the manger is clean, but abundant crops come by the strength of the ox.

5 A faithful witness does not lie, but a false witness breathes out lies.

6 A scoffer seeks wisdom in vain, but knowledge is easy for a man of understanding.

7 Leave the presence of a fool, for there you do not meet words of knowledge.

8 The wisdom of the prudent is to discern his way, but the folly of fools is deceiving.

9 Fools mock at the guilt offering, but the upright enjoy acceptance.[b]

10 The heart knows its own bitterness, and no stranger shares its joy.

11 The house of the wicked will be destroyed, but the tent of the upright will flourish.

12 There is a way that seems right to a man, but its end is the way to death.[c]

13 Even in laughter the heart may ache, and the end of joy may be grief.

14 The backslider in heart will be filled with the fruit of his ways, and a good man will be filled with the fruit of his ways.

15 The simple believes everything, but the prudent gives thought to his steps.

16 One who is wise is cautious[d] and turns away from evil, but a fool is reckless and careless.

17 A man of quick temper acts foolishly, and a man of evil devices is hated.

18 The simple inherit folly, but the prudent are crowned with knowledge.

19 The evil bow down before the good, the wicked at the gates of the righteous.

20 The poor is disliked even by his neighbor, but the rich has many friends.

21 Whoever despises his neighbor is a sinner, but blessed is he who is generous to the poor.

22 Do they not go astray who devise evil? Those who devise good meet[e] steadfast love and faithfulness.

23 In all toil there is profit, but mere talk tends only to poverty.

24 The crown of the wise is their wealth, but the folly of fools brings folly.

25 A truthful witness saves lives, but one who breathes out lies is deceitful.

26 In the fear of the Lord one has strong confidence, and his children will have a refuge.

27 The fear of the Lord is a fountain of life, that one may turn away from the snares of death.

28 In a multitude of people is the glory of a king, but without people a prince is ruined.

29 Whoever is slow to anger has great understanding, but he who has a hasty temper exalts folly.

30 A tranquil[f] heart gives life to the flesh, but envy[g] makes the bones rot.

31 Whoever oppresses a poor man insults his Maker, but he who is generous to the needy honors him.

32 The wicked is overthrown through his evildoing, but the righteous finds refuge in his death.

33 Wisdom rests in the heart of a man of understanding, but it makes itself known even in the midst of fools.[h]

34 Righteousness exalts a nation, but sin is a reproach to any people.

35 A servant who deals wisely has the king's favor, but his wrath falls on one who acts shamefully.

---

a. Proverbs 14:3 Or *In the mouth of a fool is a rod of pride* | b. Proverbs 14:9 Hebrew *but among the upright is acceptance* | c. Proverbs 14:12 Hebrew *ways of death* | d. Proverbs 14:16 Or *fears* [the Lord] | e. Proverbs 14:22 Or *show* | f. Proverbs 14:30 Or *healing* | g. Proverbs 14:30 Or *jealousy* | h. Proverbs 14:33 Or *Wisdom rests quietly in the heart of a man of understanding, but makes itself known in the midst of fools*

Notes...

Reflection Questions...

As you read today's chapter in Proverbs

1. Did a verse or group of verses catch your attention? If so, why?

   a. How can you apply this wisdom in your life today/this week?

   b. Will you make the effort to commit this verse (or verses) to memory?

2. Did you see a recurring theme?

   a. If so, why is this theme important in our lives?

   b. How could applying this wisdom change your life and/or your relationships with others?

3. Did you find something you could praise God for? Take a moment to thank Him for a few blessings today.

4. Did you find a verse that you can incorporate in your time of prayer with God?

5. Were you reminded of any mistakes that you've made in the past? Take a moment and ask the Lord to forgive you and give you the strength to walk in His ways moving forward.

Day 15
Proverbs 15

1 A soft answer turns away wrath, but a harsh word stirs up anger.

2 The tongue of the wise commends knowledge, but the mouths of fools pour out folly.

3 The eyes of the Lord are in every place, keeping watch on the evil and the good.

4 A gentle[a] tongue is a tree of life, but perverseness in it breaks the spirit.

5 A fool despises his father's instruction, but whoever heeds reproof is prudent.

6 In the house of the righteous there is much treasure, but trouble befalls the income of the wicked.

7 The lips of the wise spread knowledge; not so the hearts of fools.[b]

8 The sacrifice of the wicked is an abomination to the Lord, but the prayer of the upright is acceptable to him.

9 The way of the wicked is an abomination to the Lord, but he loves him who pursues righteousness.

10 There is severe discipline for him who forsakes the way; whoever hates reproof will die.

11 Sheol and Abaddon lie open before the Lord; how much more the hearts of the children of man!

12 A scoffer does not like to be reproved; he will not go to the wise.

13 A glad heart makes a cheerful face, but by sorrow of heart the spirit is crushed.

14 The heart of him who has understanding seeks knowledge, but the mouths of fools feed on folly.

15 All the days of the afflicted are evil, but the cheerful of heart has a continual feast.

16 Better is a little with the fear of the Lord than great treasure and trouble with it.

17 Better is a dinner of herbs where love is than a fattened ox and hatred with it.

18 A hot-tempered man stirs up strife, but he who is slow to anger quiets contention.

19 The way of a sluggard is like a hedge of thorns, but the path of the upright is a level highway.

20 A wise son makes a glad father, but a foolish man despises his mother.

21 Folly is a joy to him who lacks sense, but a man of understanding walks straight ahead.

22 Without counsel plans fail, but with many advisers they succeed.

23 To make an apt answer is a joy to a man, and a word in season, how good it is!

24 The path of life leads upward for the prudent, that he may turn away from Sheol beneath.

25 The Lord tears down the house of the proud but maintains the widow's boundaries.

26 The thoughts of the wicked are an abomination to the Lord, but gracious words are pure.

27 Whoever is greedy for unjust gain troubles his own household, but he who hates bribes will live.

28 The heart of the righteous ponders how to answer, but the mouth of the wicked pours out evil things.

29 The Lord is far from the wicked, but he hears the prayer of the righteous.

30 The light of the eyes rejoices the heart, and good news refreshes[c] the bones.

31 The ear that listens to life-giving reproof will dwell among the wise.

32 Whoever ignores instruction despises himself, but he who listens to reproof gains intelligence.

33 The fear of the Lord is instruction in wisdom, and humility comes before honor.

---

a. Proverbs 15:4 Or *healing* | b. Proverbs 15:7 Or *the hearts of fools are not steadfast* | c. Proverbs 15:30 Hebrew *makes fat*

Notes...

Reflection Questions...

As you read today's chapter in Proverbs

1. Did a verse or group of verses catch your attention? If so, why?

    ____

    ____

    a. How can you apply this wisdom in your life today/this week?

    ____

    ____

    b. Will you make the effort to commit this verse (or verses) to memory?

    ____

    ____

2. Did you see a recurring theme?

    ____

    ____

    a. If so, why is this theme important in our lives?

    ____

    ____

    b. How could applying this wisdom change your life and/or your relationships with others?

    ____

    ____

3. Did you find something you could praise God for? Take a moment to thank Him for a few blessings today.

    ____

    ____

4. Did you find a verse that you can incorporate in your time of prayer with God?

    ____

    ____

5. Were you reminded of any mistakes that you've made in the past? Take a moment and ask the Lord to forgive you and give you the strength to walk in His ways moving forward.

    ____

    ____

Day 16

Proverbs 16

1 The plans of the heart belong to man, but the answer of the tongue is from the LORD.

2 All the ways of a man are pure in his own eyes, but the LORD weighs the spirit.

3 Commit your work to the LORD, and your plans will be established.

4 The LORD has made everything for its purpose, even the wicked for the day of trouble.

5 Everyone who is arrogant in heart is an abomination to the LORD; be assured, he will not go unpunished.

6 By steadfast love and faithfulness iniquity is atoned for, and by the fear of the LORD one turns away from evil.

7 When a man's ways please the LORD, he makes even his enemies to be at peace with him.

8 Better is a little with righteousness than great revenues with injustice.

9 The heart of man plans his way, but the LORD establishes his steps.

10 An oracle is on the lips of a king; his mouth does not sin in judgment.

11 A just balance and scales are the LORD's; all the weights in the bag are his work.

12 It is an abomination to kings to do evil, for the throne is established by righteousness.

13 Righteous lips are the delight of a king, and he loves him who speaks what is right.

14 A king's wrath is a messenger of death, and a wise man will appease it.

15 In the light of a king's face there is life, and his favor is like the clouds that bring the spring rain.

16 How much better to get wisdom than gold! To get understanding is to be chosen rather than silver.

17 The highway of the upright turns aside from evil; whoever guards his way preserves his life.

18 Pride goes before destruction, and a haughty spirit before a fall.

19 It is better to be of a lowly spirit with the poor than to divide the spoil with the proud.

20 Whoever gives thought to the word[a] will discover good, and blessed is he who trusts in the Lord.

21 The wise of heart is called discerning, and sweetness of speech increases persuasiveness.

22 Good sense is a fountain of life to him who has it, but the instruction of fools is folly.

23 The heart of the wise makes his speech judicious and adds persuasiveness to his lips.

24 Gracious words are like a honeycomb, sweetness to the soul and health to the body.

25 There is a way that seems right to a man, but its end is the way to death.[b]

26 A worker's appetite works for him; his mouth urges him on.

27 A worthless man plots evil, and his speech[c] is like a scorching fire.

28 A dishonest man spreads strife, and a whisperer separates close friends.

29 A man of violence entices his neighbor and leads him in a way that is not good.

30 Whoever winks his eyes plans[d] dishonest things; he who purses his lips brings evil to pass.

31 Gray hair is a crown of glory; it is gained in a righteous life.

32 Whoever is slow to anger is better than the mighty, and he who rules his spirit than he who takes a city.

33 The lot is cast into the lap, but its every decision is from the Lord.

---

a. Proverbs 16:20 Or *to a matter* | b. Proverbs 16:25 Hebrew *ways of death* | c. Proverbs 16:27 Hebrew *what is on his lips* | d. Proverbs 16:30 Hebrew *to plan*

Notes...

Reflection Questions...

As you read today's chapter in Proverbs

1. Did a verse or group of verses catch your attention? If so, why?

    a. How can you apply this wisdom in your life today/this week?

    b. Will you make the effort to commit this verse (or verses) to memory?

2. Did you see a recurring theme?

    a. If so, why is this theme important in our lives?

    b. How could applying this wisdom change your life and/or your relationships with others?

3. Did you find something you could praise God for? Take a moment to thank Him for a few blessings today.

4. Did you find a verse that you can incorporate in your time of prayer with God?

5. Were you reminded of any mistakes that you've made in the past? Take a moment and ask the Lord to forgive you and give you the strength to walk in His ways moving forward.

Day 17

Proverbs 17

1 Better is a dry morsel with quiet than a house full of feasting[a] with strife.

2 A servant who deals wisely will rule over a son who acts shamefully and will share the inheritance as one of the brothers.

3 The crucible is for silver, and the furnace is for gold, and the Lord tests hearts.

4 An evildoer listens to wicked lips, and a liar gives ear to a mischievous tongue.

5 Whoever mocks the poor insults his Maker; he who is glad at calamity will not go unpunished.

6 Grandchildren are the crown of the aged, and the glory of children is their fathers.

7 Fine speech is not becoming to a fool; still less is false speech to a prince.

8 A bribe is like a magic stone in the eyes of the one who gives it; wherever he turns he prospers.

9 Whoever covers an offense seeks love, but he who repeats a matter separates close friends.

10 A rebuke goes deeper into a man of understanding than a hundred blows into a fool.

11 An evil man seeks only rebellion, and a cruel messenger will be sent against him.

12 Let a man meet a she-bear robbed of her cubs rather than a fool in his folly.

13 If anyone returns evil for good, evil will not depart from his house.

14 The beginning of strife is like letting out water, so quit before the quarrel breaks out.

15 He who justifies the wicked and he who condemns the righteous are both alike an abomination to the Lord.

16 Why should a fool have money in his hand to buy wisdom when he has no sense?

17 A friend loves at all times, and a brother is born for adversity.

18 One who lacks sense gives a pledge and puts up security in the presence of his neighbor.

19 Whoever loves transgression loves strife; he who makes his door high seeks destruction.

20 A man of crooked heart does not discover good, and one with a dishonest tongue falls into calamity.

21 He who sires a fool gets himself sorrow, and the father of a fool has no joy.

22 A joyful heart is good medicine, but a crushed spirit dries up the bones.

23 The wicked accepts a bribe in secret[b] to pervert the ways of justice.

24 The discerning sets his face toward wisdom, but the eyes of a fool are on the ends of the earth.

25 A foolish son is a grief to his father and bitterness to her who bore him.

26 To impose a fine on a righteous man is not good, nor to strike the noble for their uprightness.

27 Whoever restrains his words has knowledge, and he who has a cool spirit is a man of understanding.

28 Even a fool who keeps silent is considered wise; when he closes his lips, he is deemed intelligent.

---

a. Proverbs 17:1 Hebrew *sacrifices* | b. Proverbs 17:23 Hebrew *a bribe from the bosom*

Notes...

Reflection Questions...

As you read today's chapter in Proverbs

1. Did a verse or group of verses catch your attention? If so, why?

    a. How can you apply this wisdom in your life today/this week?

    b. Will you make the effort to commit this verse (or verses) to memory?

2. Did you see a recurring theme?

    a. If so, why is this theme important in our lives?

    b. How could applying this wisdom change your life and/or your relationships with others?

3. Did you find something you could praise God for? Take a moment to thank Him for a few blessings today.

4. Did you find a verse that you can incorporate in your time of prayer with God?

5. Were you reminded of any mistakes that you've made in the past? Take a moment and ask the Lord to forgive you and give you the strength to walk in His ways moving forward.

Day 18
Proverbs 18

1 Whoever isolates himself seeks his own desire; he breaks out against all sound judgment.

2 A fool takes no pleasure in understanding, but only in expressing his opinion.

3 When wickedness comes, contempt comes also, and with dishonor comes disgrace.

4 The words of a man's mouth are deep waters; the fountain of wisdom is a bubbling brook.

5 It is not good to be partial to[a] the wicked or to deprive the righteous of justice.

6 A fool's lips walk into a fight, and his mouth invites a beating.

7 A fool's mouth is his ruin, and his lips are a snare to his soul.

8 The words of a whisperer are like delicious morsels; they go down into the inner parts of the body.

9 Whoever is slack in his work is a brother to him who destroys.

10 The name of the Lord is a strong tower; the righteous man runs into it and is safe.

11 A rich man's wealth is his strong city, and like a high wall in his imagination.

12 Before destruction a man's heart is haughty, but humility comes before honor.

13 If one gives an answer before he hears, it is his folly and shame.

14 A man's spirit will endure sickness, but a crushed spirit who can bear?

15 An intelligent heart acquires knowledge, and the ear of the wise seeks knowledge.

16 A man's gift makes room for him and brings him before the great.

17 The one who states his case first seems right, until the other comes and examines him.

18 The lot puts an end to quarrels and decides between powerful contenders.

19 A brother offended is more unyielding than a strong city, and quarreling is like the bars of a castle.

20 From the fruit of a man's mouth his stomach is satisfied; he is satisfied by the yield of his lips.

21 Death and life are in the power of the tongue, and those who love it will eat its fruits.

22 He who finds a wife finds a good thing and obtains favor from the LORD.

23 The poor use entreaties, but the rich answer roughly.

24 A man of many companions may come to ruin, but there is a friend who sticks closer than a brother.

---

a. Proverbs 18:5 Hebrew *to lift the face of*

Notes...

Reflection Questions...

As you read today's chapter in Proverbs

1. Did a verse or group of verses catch your attention? If so, why?

   ____

   ____

   a. How can you apply this wisdom in your life today/this week?

      ____

      ____

   b. Will you make the effort to commit this verse (or verses) to memory?

      ____

      ____

2. Did you see a recurring theme?

   ____

   ____

   a. If so, why is this theme important in our lives?

      ____

      ____

   b. How could applying this wisdom change your life and/or your relationships with others?

      ____

      ____

3. Did you find something you could praise God for? Take a moment to thank Him for a few blessings today.

   ____

   ____

4. Did you find a verse that you can incorporate in your time of prayer with God?

   ____

   ____

5. Were you reminded of any mistakes that you've made in the past? Take a moment and ask the Lord to forgive you and give you the strength to walk in His ways moving forward.

   ____

   ____

Meet Wisdom

A Walk to Wisdom was not compiled just to help you increase your knowledge base or intellectual capacity as you may have originally thought. It was also designed to introduce you to the One who is the wisdom of God, Christ Jesus. The Scripture, 1 Corinthians 1:24 tells us this, *"but to those who are called, both Jews and Greeks, Christ the power of God and the wisdom of God."* What an amazing statement! Jesus Himself is the wisdom you have been searching for in your life and in this book. Truly, as we learn in Colossians, all the treasures of wisdom and knowledge are hidden in Christ. Stop and think about that for a moment. Whatever motivates you to seek after wisdom and stirs your heart to search for knowledge, Jesus not only has the answer, He is the answer. All of the purpose and joy and love and peace you desire to have are found in Him! I now understand why my own father signed my Bible years ago with these words: "As your life unfolds, remember—all the answers are in Christ." What better advice could a father give his son?

The Bible tells us that He (Jesus) *"became to us wisdom from God, righteousness and sanctification and redemption . . ." (1 Corinthians 1:30)*. These are unfamiliar words to us I know, but this is a summary of the gospel message. When we were in the wrong, He covered us in His "rightness"; when we were selfish and full of our wicked ways, He sanctified us and set us apart; when we were dead in our sins, He bought us back with His blood on the cross and furthermore He conquered death by His resurrection. What better news is there in all the world?

You and I intuitively know this to be true; let your conscience confirm it for a moment. After reading through the first half of Proverbs, how many times did you feel the weight of guilt from your past mistakes or wrong choices you've made over the years? How many times did the Scriptures pierce your heart and convict your mind of previous blunders along life's way? As you began to understand how God really wants us to live and to love others, didn't you feel a bit unworthy or unable to do so on your own? This is the very reason that Jesus came; to pay a debt we couldn't pay, to cleanse our consciences and remove our guilt, to reconcile us back into a relationship with our Father in heaven that our sins had broken apart, and give us the ability to walk in truth and love. This is why the gospel is called good news! This is something we could never do on our own but Jesus, God's only begotten Son, the Righteous and sinless One, He did it for us.

He willingly and joyfully endured the cross for our benefit and He is the only one qualified to do so! What greater love is there in all the world! Hear the message and heed the call, *"that Christ died for our sins in accordance with the Scriptures, that he was buried, that he was raised on the third day in accordance with the Scriptures, and that he appeared to Cephas, then to the twelve. Then he appeared to more than five hundred brothers at one time . . ." (1 Corinthians 15:3b–6a)*

Here is the bad news, *"it is appointed for man to die once, and after that comes judgment" (Hebrews 9:27).* We will all stand before God, the Just Judge, who knows all and sees all, and we will have to give an account for everything we have said and done. Apart from Christ, we stand guilty before Him as our consciences have confirmed and the Word of God makes clear. And yet, Jesus has paid our debt in full! He died for you, He rose for you, and He lives to intercede for you. He will cover you in His righteousness if you are willing to repent of your sins and trust and obey Him. If you have never put your faith in Jesus Christ as your Savior and Lord, I ask you, dare I beg you, to do so right now. You may not live until tomorrow or Jesus may come back tonight. There is no magic formula; there is not a perfect prayer but the gospel which you have just heard is *"the power of God for salvation to everyone who believes" (Romans 1:16).* Believe then in Christ Jesus and you will be saved! Put your faith and trust in Him and ask Him to forgive you of all of your sins and fill you with the Holy Spirit even now, so that you can walk in the light of His presence and strength.

If you have just given your life to Christ, welcome to the family of God! Know that He has prepared good works in advance for you to do, and you will find the greatest joy and fulfillment in life as you walk in these ways. I highly encourage you to search for a biblically based church in your area, meet with the pastor, and speak with him about baptism and what it means to sincerely follow Jesus and walk in His ways. Your new life is just beginning. This is not a finish line, but rather the first (and the greatest) step of faith in a lifelong walk with Jesus who is the *"friend who sticks closer than a brother"* that you just read about in Proverbs eighteen. He will never leave you, He will never forsake you, and He is with you wherever you go. What wonderful promises we have in Christ Jesus!

If you have any questions or would like to speak to a pastor or someone about your recent decision, please contact Von Minor or his staff at Restoration Church at 469-621-5910 or vminor@rccdallas.org.

You can also reach me at trogtrogdon@gmail.com.

Day 19

Proverbs 19

1 Better is a poor person who walks in his integrity than one who is crooked in speech and is a fool.

2 Desire[a] without knowledge is not good, and whoever makes haste with his feet misses his way.

3 When a man's folly brings his way to ruin, his heart rages against the Lord.

4 Wealth brings many new friends, but a poor man is deserted by his friend.

5 A false witness will not go unpunished, and he who breathes out lies will not escape.

6 Many seek the favor of a generous man,[b] and everyone is a friend to a man who gives gifts.

7 All a poor man's brothers hate him; how much more do his friends go far from him! He pursues them with words, but does not have them.[c]

8 Whoever gets sense loves his own soul; he who keeps understanding will discover good.

9 A false witness will not go unpunished, and he who breathes out lies will perish.

10 It is not fitting for a fool to live in luxury, much less for a slave to rule over princes.

11 Good sense makes one slow to anger, and it is his glory to overlook an offense.

12 A king's wrath is like the growling of a lion, but his favor is like dew on the grass.

13 A foolish son is ruin to his father, and a wife's quarreling is a continual dripping of rain.

14 House and wealth are inherited from fathers, but a prudent wife is from the Lord.

15 Slothfulness casts into a deep sleep, and an idle person will suffer hunger.

16 Whoever keeps the commandment keeps his life; he who despises his ways will die.

17 Whoever is generous to the poor lends to the Lord, and he will repay him for his deed.

18 Discipline your son, for there is hope; do not set your heart on putting him to death.

19 A man of great wrath will pay the penalty, for if you deliver him, you will only have to do it again.

20 Listen to advice and accept instruction, that you may gain wisdom in the future.

21 Many are the plans in the mind of a man, but it is the purpose of the Lord that will stand.

22 What is desired in a man is steadfast love, and a poor man is better than a liar.

23 The fear of the Lord leads to life, and whoever has it rests satisfied; he will not be visited by harm.

24 The sluggard buries his hand in the dish and will not even bring it back to his mouth.

25 Strike a scoffer, and the simple will learn prudence; reprove a man of understanding, and he will gain knowledge.

26 He who does violence to his father and chases away his mother is a son who brings shame and reproach.

27 Cease to hear instruction, my son, and you will stray from the words of knowledge.

28 A worthless witness mocks at justice, and the mouth of the wicked devours iniquity.

29 Condemnation is ready for scoffers, and beating for the backs of fools.

---

a. Proverbs 19:2 Or *A soul* | b. Proverbs 19:6 Or *of a noble* | c. Proverbs 19:7 The meaning of the Hebrew sentence is uncertain

Notes...

Reflection Questions...

As you read today's chapter in Proverbs

1. Did a verse or group of verses catch your attention? If so, why?

   a. How can you apply this wisdom in your life today/this week?

   b. Will you make the effort to commit this verse (or verses) to memory?

2. Did you see a recurring theme?

   a. If so, why is this theme important in our lives?

   b. How could applying this wisdom change your life and/or your relationships with others?

3. Did you find something you could praise God for? Take a moment to thank Him for a few blessings today.

4. Did you find a verse that you can incorporate in your time of prayer with God?

5. Were you reminded of any mistakes that you've made in the past? Take a moment and ask the Lord to forgive you and give you the strength to walk in His ways moving forward.

Day 20

Proverbs 20

1 Wine is a mocker, strong drink a brawler, and whoever is led astray by it is not wise.[a]

2 The terror of a king is like the growling of a lion; whoever provokes him to anger forfeits his life.

3 It is an honor for a man to keep aloof from strife, but every fool will be quarreling.

4 The sluggard does not plow in the autumn; he will seek at harvest and have nothing.

5 The purpose in a man's heart is like deep water, but a man of understanding will draw it out.

6 Many a man proclaims his own steadfast love, but a faithful man who can find?

7 The righteous who walks in his integrity—blessed are his children after him!

8 A king who sits on the throne of judgment winnows all evil with his eyes.

9 Who can say, "I have made my heart pure; I am clean from my sin"?

10 Unequal[b] weights and unequal measures are both alike an abomination to the Lord.

11 Even a child makes himself known by his acts, by whether his conduct is pure and upright.[c]

12 The hearing ear and the seeing eye, the Lord has made them both.

13 Love not sleep, lest you come to poverty; open your eyes, and you will have plenty of bread.

14 "Bad, bad," says the buyer, but when he goes away, then he boasts.

15 There is gold and abundance of costly stones, but the lips of knowledge are a precious jewel.

16 Take a man's garment when he has put up security for a stranger, and hold it in pledge when he puts up security for foreigners.[d]

17 Bread gained by deceit is sweet to a man, but afterward his mouth will be full of gravel.

18 Plans are established by counsel; by wise guidance wage war.

19 Whoever goes about slandering reveals secrets; therefore do not associate with a simple babbler.[e]

20 If one curses his father or his mother, his lamp will be put out in utter darkness.

21 An inheritance gained hastily in the beginning will not be blessed in the end.

22 Do not say, "I will repay evil"; wait for the Lord, and he will deliver you.

23 Unequal weights are an abomination to the Lord, and false scales are not good.

24 A man's steps are from the Lord; how then can man understand his way?

25 It is a snare to say rashly, "It is holy," and to reflect only after making vows.

26 A wise king winnows the wicked and drives the wheel over them.

27 The spirit[f] of man is the lamp of the Lord, searching all his innermost parts.

28 Steadfast love and faithfulness preserve the king, and by steadfast love his throne is upheld.

29 The glory of young men is their strength, but the splendor of old men is their gray hair.

30 Blows that wound cleanse away evil; strokes make clean the innermost parts.

---

a. Proverbs 20:1 Or *will not become wise* | b. Proverbs 20:10 Or *Two kinds of*; also verse 23 | c. Proverbs 20:11 Or *Even a child can dissemble in his actions, though his conduct seems pure and upright.* | d. Proverbs 20:16 Or *for an adulteress* (compare 27:13) | e. Proverbs 20:19 Hebrew *with one who is simple in his lips* | f. Proverbs 20:27 Hebrew *breath*

Notes...

Reflection Questions...

As you read today's chapter in Proverbs

1. Did a verse or group of verses catch your attention? If so, why?

   a. How can you apply this wisdom in your life today/this week?

   b. Will you make the effort to commit this verse (or verses) to memory?

2. Did you see a recurring theme?

   a. If so, why is this theme important in our lives?

   b. How could applying this wisdom change your life and/or your relationships with others?

3. Did you find something you could praise God for? Take a moment to thank Him for a few blessings today.

4. Did you find a verse that you can incorporate in your time of prayer with God?

5. Were you reminded of any mistakes that you've made in the past? Take a moment and ask the Lord to forgive you and give you the strength to walk in His ways moving forward.

Day 21
Proverbs 21

1 The king's heart is a stream of water in the hand of the Lord; he turns it wherever he will.

2 Every way of a man is right in his own eyes, but the Lord weighs the heart.

3 To do righteousness and justice is more acceptable to the Lord than sacrifice.

4 Haughty eyes and a proud heart, the lamp[a] of the wicked, are sin.

5 The plans of the diligent lead surely to abundance, but everyone who is hasty comes only to poverty.

6 The getting of treasures by a lying tongue is a fleeting vapor and a snare of death.[b]

7 The violence of the wicked will sweep them away, because they refuse to do what is just.

8 The way of the guilty is crooked, but the conduct of the pure is upright.

9 It is better to live in a corner of the housetop than in a house shared with a quarrelsome wife.

10 The soul of the wicked desires evil; his neighbor finds no mercy in his eyes.

11 When a scoffer is punished, the simple becomes wise; when a wise man is instructed, he gains knowledge.

12 The Righteous One observes the house of the wicked; he throws the wicked down to ruin.

13 Whoever closes his ear to the cry of the poor will himself call out and not be answered.

14 A gift in secret averts anger, and a concealed bribe,[c] strong wrath.

15 When justice is done, it is a joy to the righteous but terror to evildoers.

16 One who wanders from the way of good sense will rest in the assembly of the dead.

17 Whoever loves pleasure will be a poor man; he who loves wine and oil will not be rich.

18 The wicked is a ransom for the righteous, and the traitor for the upright.

19 It is better to live in a desert land than with a quarrelsome and fretful woman.

20 Precious treasure and oil are in a wise man's dwelling, but a foolish man devours it.

21 Whoever pursues righteousness and kindness will find life, righteousness, and honor.

22 A wise man scales the city of the mighty and brings down the stronghold in which they trust.

23 Whoever keeps his mouth and his tongue keeps himself out of trouble.

24 "Scoffer" is the name of the arrogant, haughty man who acts with arrogant pride.

25 The desire of the sluggard kills him, for his hands refuse to labor.

26 All day long he craves and craves, but the righteous gives and does not hold back.

27 The sacrifice of the wicked is an abomination; how much more when he brings it with evil intent.

28 A false witness will perish, but the word of a man who hears will endure.

29 A wicked man puts on a bold face, but the upright gives thought to[d] his ways.

30 No wisdom, no understanding, no counsel can avail against the Lord.

31 The horse is made ready for the day of battle, but the victory belongs to the Lord.

---

a. Proverbs 21:4 Or *the plowing* | b. Proverbs 21:6 Some Hebrew manuscripts, Septuagint, Latin; most Hebrew manuscripts *vapor for those who seek death* | c. Proverbs 21:14 Hebrew *a bribe in the bosom* | d. Proverbs 21:29 Or *establishes*

Notes...

Reflection Questions...

As you read today's chapter in Proverbs

1. Did a verse or group of verses catch your attention? If so, why?

    a. How can you apply this wisdom in your life today/this week?

    b. Will you make the effort to commit this verse (or verses) to memory?

2. Did you see a recurring theme?

    a. If so, why is this theme important in our lives?

    b. How could applying this wisdom change your life and/or your relationships with others?

3. Did you find something you could praise God for? Take a moment to thank Him for a few blessings today.

4. Did you find a verse that you can incorporate in your time of prayer with God?

5. Were you reminded of any mistakes that you've made in the past? Take a moment and ask the Lord to forgive you and give you the strength to walk in His ways moving forward.

Notes...

Reflection Questions...

As you read today's chapter in Proverbs

1. Did a verse or group of verses catch your attention? If so, why?

    a. How can you apply this wisdom in your life today/this week?

    b. Will you make the effort to commit this verse (or verses) to memory?

2. Did you see a recurring theme?

    a. If so, why is this theme important in our lives?

    b. How could applying this wisdom change your life and/or your relationships with others?

3. Did you find something you could praise God for? Take a moment to thank Him for a few blessings today.

4. Did you find a verse that you can incorporate in your time of prayer with God?

5. Were you reminded of any mistakes that you've made in the past? Take a moment and ask the Lord to forgive you and give you the strength to walk in His ways moving forward.

Day 23

Proverbs 23

1 When you sit down to eat with a ruler, observe carefully what[a] is before you,

2 and put a knife to your throat if you are given to appetite.

3 Do not desire his delicacies, for they are deceptive food.

4 Do not toil to acquire wealth; be discerning enough to desist.

5 When your eyes light on it, it is gone, for suddenly it sprouts wings, flying like an eagle toward heaven.

6 Do not eat the bread of a man who is stingy;[b] do not desire his delicacies,

7 for he is like one who is inwardly calculating.[c] "Eat and drink!" he says to you, but his heart is not with you.

8 You will vomit up the morsels that you have eaten, and waste your pleasant words.

9 Do not speak in the hearing of a fool, for he will despise the good sense of your words.

10 Do not move an ancient landmark or enter the fields of the fatherless,

11 for their Redeemer is strong; he will plead their cause against you.

12 Apply your heart to instruction and your ear to words of knowledge.

13 Do not withhold discipline from a child; if you strike him with a rod, he will not die.

14 If you strike him with the rod, you will save his soul from Sheol.

15 My son, if your heart is wise, my heart too will be glad.

16 My inmost being[d] will exult when your lips speak what is right.

17 Let not your heart envy sinners, but continue in the fear of the Lord all the day.

18 Surely there is a future, and your hope will not be cut off.

19 Hear, my son, and be wise, and direct your heart in the way.

20 Be not among drunkards[e] or among gluttonous eaters of meat,

21 for the drunkard and the glutton will come to poverty, and slumber will clothe them with rags.

22 Listen to your father who gave you life, and do not despise your mother when she is old.

23 Buy truth, and do not sell it; buy wisdom, instruction, and understanding.

24 The father of the righteous will greatly rejoice; he who fathers a wise son will be glad in him.

25 Let your father and mother be glad; let her who bore you rejoice.

26 My son, give me your heart, and let your eyes observe[f] my ways.

27 For a prostitute is a deep pit; an adulteress[g] is a narrow well.

28 She lies in wait like a robber and increases the traitors among mankind.

29 Who has woe? Who has sorrow? Who has strife? Who has complaining? Who has wounds without cause? Who has redness of eyes?

30 Those who tarry long over wine; those who go to try mixed wine.

31 Do not look at wine when it is red, when it sparkles in the cup and goes down smoothly.

32 In the end it bites like a serpent and stings like an adder.

33 Your eyes will see strange things, and your heart utter perverse things.

34 You will be like one who lies down in the midst of the sea, like one who lies on the top of a mast.[h]

35 "They struck me," you will say,[i] "but I was not hurt; they beat me, but I did not feel it. When shall I awake? I must have another drink."

---

a. Proverbs 23:1 Or *who* | b. Proverbs 23:6 Hebrew *whose eye is evil* | c. Proverbs 23:7 Or *for as he calculates in his soul, so is he* | d. Proverbs 23:16 Hebrew *My kidneys* | e. Proverbs 23:20 Hebrew *those who drink too much wine* | f. Proverbs 23:26 Or *delight in* | g. Proverbs 23:27 Hebrew *a foreign woman* | h. Proverbs 23:34 Or *of the rigging* | i. Proverbs 23:35 Hebrew lacks *you will say*

Notes...

Reflection Questions...

As you read today's chapter in Proverbs

1. Did a verse or group of verses catch your attention? If so, why?

   a. How can you apply this wisdom in your life today/this week?

   b. Will you make the effort to commit this verse (or verses) to memory?

2. Did you see a recurring theme?

   a. If so, why is this theme important in our lives?

   b. How could applying this wisdom change your life and/or your relationships with others?

3. Did you find something you could praise God for? Take a moment to thank Him for a few blessings today.

4. Did you find a verse that you can incorporate in your time of prayer with God?

5. Were you reminded of any mistakes that you've made in the past? Take a moment and ask the Lord to forgive you and give you the strength to walk in His ways moving forward.

Day 24

Proverbs 24

1 Be not envious of evil men, nor desire to be with them,

2 for their hearts devise violence, and their lips talk of trouble.

3 By wisdom a house is built, and by understanding it is established;

4 by knowledge the rooms are filled with all precious and pleasant riches.

5 A wise man is full of strength, and a man of knowledge enhances his might,

6 for by wise guidance you can wage your war, and in abundance of counselors there is victory.

7 Wisdom is too high for a fool; in the gate he does not open his mouth.

8 Whoever plans to do evil will be called a schemer.

9 The devising[a] of folly is sin, and the scoffer is an abomination to mankind.

10 If you faint in the day of adversity, your strength is small.

11 Rescue those who are being taken away to death; hold back those who are stumbling to the slaughter.

12 If you say, "Behold, we did not know this," does not he who weighs the heart perceive it? Does not he who keeps watch over your soul know it, and will he not repay man according to his work?

13 My son, eat honey, for it is good, and the drippings of the honeycomb are sweet to your taste.

14 Know that wisdom is such to your soul; if you find it, there will be a future, and your hope will not be cut off.

15 Lie not in wait as a wicked man against the dwelling of the righteous; do no violence to his home;

16 for the righteous falls seven times and rises again, but the wicked stumble in times of calamity.

17 Do not rejoice when your enemy falls, and let not your heart be glad when he stumbles,

18 lest the Lord see it and be displeased, and turn away his anger from him.

19 Fret not yourself because of evildoers, and be not envious of the wicked,

20 for the evil man has no future; the lamp of the wicked will be put out.

21 My son, fear the LORD and the king, and do not join with those who do otherwise,

22 for disaster will arise suddenly from them, and who knows the ruin that will come from them both?

More Sayings of the Wise

23 These also are sayings of the wise. Partiality in judging is not good.

24 Whoever says to the wicked, "You are in the right," will be cursed by peoples, abhorred by nations,

25 but those who rebuke the wicked will have delight, and a good blessing will come upon them.

26 Whoever gives an honest answer kisses the lips.

27 Prepare your work outside; get everything ready for yourself in the field, and after that build your house.

28 Be not a witness against your neighbor without cause, and do not deceive with your lips.

29 Do not say, "I will do to him as he has done to me; I will pay the man back for what he has done."

30 I passed by the field of a sluggard, by the vineyard of a man lacking sense,

31 and behold, it was all overgrown with thorns; the ground was covered with nettles, and its stone wall was broken down.

32 Then I saw and considered it; I looked and received instruction.

33 A little sleep, a little slumber, a little folding of the hands to rest,

34 and poverty will come upon you like a robber, and want like an armed man.

---

a. Proverbs 24:9 Or *scheming*

Notes...

Reflection Questions...

As you read today's chapter in Proverbs

1. Did a verse or group of verses catch your attention? If so, why?

    a. How can you apply this wisdom in your life today/this week?

    b. Will you make the effort to commit this verse (or verses) to memory?

2. Did you see a recurring theme?

    a. If so, why is this theme important in our lives?

    b. How could applying this wisdom change your life and/or your relationships with others?

3. Did you find something you could praise God for? Take a moment to thank Him for a few blessings today.

4. Did you find a verse that you can incorporate in your time of prayer with God?

5. Were you reminded of any mistakes that you've made in the past? Take a moment and ask the Lord to forgive you and give you the strength to walk in His ways moving forward.

Day 25

Proverbs 25

More Proverbs of Solomon

1 These also are proverbs of Solomon which the men of Hezekiah king of Judah copied.

2 It is the glory of God to conceal things, but the glory of kings is to search things out.

3 As the heavens for height, and the earth for depth, so the heart of kings is unsearchable.

4 Take away the dross from the silver, and the smith has material for a vessel;

5 take away the wicked from the presence of the king, and his throne will be established in righteousness.

6 Do not put yourself forward in the king's presence or stand in the place of the great,

7 for it is better to be told, "Come up here," than to be put lower in the presence of a noble. What your eyes have seen

8 do not hastily bring into court, for[a] what will you do in the end, when your neighbor puts you to shame?

9 Argue your case with your neighbor himself, and do not reveal another's secret,

10 lest he who hears you bring shame upon you, and your ill repute have no end.

11 A word fitly spoken is like apples of gold in a setting of silver.

12 Like a gold ring or an ornament of gold is a wise reprover to a listening ear.

13 Like the cold of snow in the time of harvest is a faithful messenger to those who send him; he refreshes the soul of his masters.

14 Like clouds and wind without rain is a man who boasts of a gift he does not give.

15 With patience a ruler may be persuaded, and a soft tongue will break a bone.

16 If you have found honey, eat only enough for you, lest you have your fill of it and vomit it.

17 Let your foot be seldom in your neighbor's house, lest he have his fill of you and hate you.

18 A man who bears false witness against his neighbor is like a war club, or a sword, or a sharp arrow.

19 Trusting in a treacherous man in time of trouble is like a bad tooth or a foot that slips.

20 Whoever sings songs to a heavy heart is like one who takes off a garment on a cold day, and like vinegar on soda.

21 If your enemy is hungry, give him bread to eat, and if he is thirsty, give him water to drink,

22 for you will heap burning coals on his head, and the Lord will reward you.

23 The north wind brings forth rain, and a backbiting tongue, angry looks.

24 It is better to live in a corner of the housetop than in a house shared with a quarrelsome wife.

25 Like cold water to a thirsty soul, so is good news from a far country.

26 Like a muddied spring or a polluted fountain is a righteous man who gives way before the wicked.

27 It is not good to eat much honey, nor is it glorious to seek one's own glory.[b]

28 A man without self-control is like a city broken into and left without walls.

---

a. Proverbs 25:8 Hebrew *or else* | b. Proverbs 25:27 The meaning of the Hebrew line is uncertain

Notes...

Reflection Questions...

As you read today's chapter in Proverbs

1. Did a verse or group of verses catch your attention? If so, why?

    a. How can you apply this wisdom in your life today/this week?

    b. Will you make the effort to commit this verse (or verses) to memory?

2. Did you see a recurring theme?

    a. If so, why is this theme important in our lives?

    b. How could applying this wisdom change your life and/or your relationships with others?

3. Did you find something you could praise God for? Take a moment to thank Him for a few blessings today.

4. Did you find a verse that you can incorporate in your time of prayer with God?

5. Were you reminded of any mistakes that you've made in the past? Take a moment and ask the Lord to forgive you and give you the strength to walk in His ways moving forward.

Day 26

Proverbs 26

1 Like snow in summer or rain in harvest, so honor is not fitting for a fool.

2 Like a sparrow in its flitting, like a swallow in its flying, a curse that is causeless does not alight.

3 A whip for the horse, a bridle for the donkey, and a rod for the back of fools.

4 Answer not a fool according to his folly, lest you be like him yourself.

5 Answer a fool according to his folly, lest he be wise in his own eyes.

6 Whoever sends a message by the hand of a fool cuts off his own feet and drinks violence.

7 Like a lame man's legs, which hang useless, is a proverb in the mouth of fools.

8 Like one who binds the stone in the sling is one who gives honor to a fool.

9 Like a thorn that goes up into the hand of a drunkard is a proverb in the mouth of fools.

10 Like an archer who wounds everyone is one who hires a passing fool or drunkard.[a]

11 Like a dog that returns to his vomit is a fool who repeats his folly.

12 Do you see a man who is wise in his own eyes? There is more hope for a fool than for him.

13 The sluggard says, "There is a lion in the road! There is a lion in the streets!"

14 As a door turns on its hinges, so does a sluggard on his bed.

15 The sluggard buries his hand in the dish; it wears him out to bring it back to his mouth.

16 The sluggard is wiser in his own eyes than seven men who can answer sensibly.

17 Whoever meddles in a quarrel not his own is like one who takes a passing dog by the ears.

18 Like a madman who throws firebrands, arrows, and death

19 is the man who deceives his neighbor and says, "I am only joking!"

20 For lack of wood the fire goes out, and where there is no whisperer, quarreling ceases.

21 As charcoal to hot embers and wood to fire, so is a quarrelsome man for kindling strife.

22 The words of a whisperer are like delicious morsels; they go down into the inner parts of the body.

23 Like the glaze[b] covering an earthen vessel are fervent lips with an evil heart.

24 Whoever hates disguises himself with his lips and harbors deceit in his heart;

25 when he speaks graciously, believe him not, for there are seven abominations in his heart;

26 though his hatred be covered with deception, his wickedness will be exposed in the assembly.

27 Whoever digs a pit will fall into it, and a stone will come back on him who starts it rolling.

28 A lying tongue hates its victims, and a flattering mouth works ruin.

---

a. Proverbs 26:10 Or *hires a fool or passersby* | b. Proverbs 26:23 By revocalization; Hebrew *silver of dross*

Notes...

Reflection Questions...

As you read today's chapter in Proverbs

1. Did a verse or group of verses catch your attention? If so, why?

   a. How can you apply this wisdom in your life today/this week?

   b. Will you make the effort to commit this verse (or verses) to memory?

2. Did you see a recurring theme?

   a. If so, why is this theme important in our lives?

   b. How could applying this wisdom change your life and/or your relationships with others?

3. Did you find something you could praise God for? Take a moment to thank Him for a few blessings today.

4. Did you find a verse that you can incorporate in your time of prayer with God?

5. Were you reminded of any mistakes that you've made in the past? Take a moment and ask the Lord to forgive you and give you the strength to walk in His ways moving forward.

Day 27
Proverbs 27

1 Do not boast about tomorrow, for you do not know what a day may bring.

2 Let another praise you, and not your own mouth; a stranger, and not your own lips.

3 A stone is heavy, and sand is weighty, but a fool's provocation is heavier than both.

4 Wrath is cruel, anger is overwhelming, but who can stand before jealousy?

5 Better is open rebuke than hidden love.

6 Faithful are the wounds of a friend; profuse are the kisses of an enemy.

7 One who is full loathes honey, but to one who is hungry everything bitter is sweet.

8 Like a bird that strays from its nest is a man who strays from his home.

9 Oil and perfume make the heart glad, and the sweetness of a friend comes from his earnest counsel.[a]

10 Do not forsake your friend and your father's friend, and do not go to your brother's house in the day of your calamity. Better is a neighbor who is near than a brother who is far away.

11 Be wise, my son, and make my heart glad, that I may answer him who reproaches me.

12 The prudent sees danger and hides himself, but the simple go on and suffer for it.

13 Take a man's garment when he has put up security for a stranger, and hold it in pledge when he puts up security for an adulteress.[b]

14 Whoever blesses his neighbor with a loud voice, rising early in the morning, will be counted as cursing.

15 A continual dripping on a rainy day and a quarrelsome wife are alike;

16 to restrain her is to restrain the wind or to grasp[c] oil in one's right hand.

17 Iron sharpens iron, and one man sharpens another.[d]

18 Whoever tends a fig tree will eat its fruit, and he who guards his master will be honored.

19 As in water face reflects face, so the heart of man reflects the man.

20 Sheol and Abaddon are never satisfied, and never satisfied are the eyes of man.

21 The crucible is for silver, and the furnace is for gold, and a man is tested by his praise.

22 Crush a fool in a mortar with a pestle along with crushed grain, yet his folly will not depart from him.

23 Know well the condition of your flocks, and give attention to your herds,

24 for riches do not last forever; and does a crown endure to all generations?

25 When the grass is gone and the new growth appears and the vegetation of the mountains is gathered,

26 the lambs will provide your clothing, and the goats the price of a field.

27 There will be enough goats' milk for your food, for the food of your household and maintenance for your girls.

---

a. Proverbs 27:9 Or *and so does the sweetness of a friend that comes from his earnest counsel* | b. Proverbs 27:13 Hebrew *a foreign woman*; a slight emendation yields (compare Vulgate; see also 20:16) *foreigners* | c. Proverbs 27:16 Hebrew *to meet with* | d. Proverbs 27:17 Hebrew *sharpens the face of another*

Notes...

Reflection Questions...

As you read today's chapter in Proverbs

1. Did a verse or group of verses catch your attention? If so, why?

    a. How can you apply this wisdom in your life today/this week?

    b. Will you make the effort to commit this verse (or verses) to memory?

2. Did you see a recurring theme?

    a. If so, why is this theme important in our lives?

    b. How could applying this wisdom change your life and/or your relationships with others?

3. Did you find something you could praise God for? Take a moment to thank Him for a few blessings today.

4. Did you find a verse that you can incorporate in your time of prayer with God?

5. Were you reminded of any mistakes that you've made in the past? Take a moment and ask the Lord to forgive you and give you the strength to walk in His ways moving forward.

Day 28

Proverbs 28

1 The wicked flee when no one pursues, but the righteous are bold as a lion.

2 When a land transgresses, it has many rulers, but with a man of understanding and knowledge, its stability will long continue.

3 A poor man who oppresses the poor is a beating rain that leaves no food.

4 Those who forsake the law praise the wicked, but those who keep the law strive against them.

5 Evil men do not understand justice, but those who seek the Lord understand it completely.

6 Better is a poor man who walks in his integrity than a rich man who is crooked in his ways.

7 The one who keeps the law is a son with understanding, but a companion of gluttons shames his father.

8 Whoever multiplies his wealth by interest and profit[a] gathers it for him who is generous to the poor.

9 If one turns away his ear from hearing the law, even his prayer is an abomination.

10 Whoever misleads the upright into an evil way will fall into his own pit, but the blameless will have a goodly inheritance.

11 A rich man is wise in his own eyes, but a poor man who has understanding will find him out.

12 When the righteous triumph, there is great glory, but when the wicked rise, people hide themselves.

13 Whoever conceals his transgressions will not prosper, but he who confesses and forsakes them will obtain mercy.

14 Blessed is the one who fears the Lord always, but whoever hardens his heart will fall into calamity.

15 Like a roaring lion or a charging bear is a wicked ruler over a poor people.

16 A ruler who lacks understanding is a cruel oppressor, but he who hates unjust gain will prolong his days.

17 If one is burdened with the blood of another, he will be a fugitive until death;[b] let no one help him.

18 Whoever walks in integrity will be delivered, but he who is crooked in his ways will suddenly fall.

19 Whoever works his land will have plenty of bread, but he who follows worthless pursuits will have plenty of poverty.

20 A faithful man will abound with blessings, but whoever hastens to be rich will not go unpunished.

21 To show partiality is not good, but for a piece of bread a man will do wrong.

22 A stingy man[c] hastens after wealth and does not know that poverty will come upon him.

23 Whoever rebukes a man will afterward find more favor than he who flatters with his tongue.

24 Whoever robs his father or his mother and says, "That is no transgression," is a companion to a man who destroys.

25 A greedy man stirs up strife, but the one who trusts in the LORD will be enriched.

26 Whoever trusts in his own mind is a fool, but he who walks in wisdom will be delivered.

27 Whoever gives to the poor will not want, but he who hides his eyes will get many a curse.

28 When the wicked rise, people hide themselves, but when they perish, the righteous increase.

---

a. Proverbs 28:8 That is, profit that comes from charging interest to the poor | b. Proverbs 28:17 Hebrew *until the pit* | c. Proverbs 28:22 Hebrew *A man whose eye is evil*

Notes...

Reflection Questions...

As you read today's chapter in Proverbs

1. Did a verse or group of verses catch your attention? If so, why?

   ____

   ____

   a. How can you apply this wisdom in your life today/this week?

      ____

      ____

   b. Will you make the effort to commit this verse (or verses) to memory?

      ____

      ____

2. Did you see a recurring theme?

   ____

   ____

   a. If so, why is this theme important in our lives?

      ____

      ____

   b. How could applying this wisdom change your life and/or your relationships with others?

      ____

      ____

3. Did you find something you could praise God for? Take a moment to thank Him for a few blessings today.

   ____

   ____

4. Did you find a verse that you can incorporate in your time of prayer with God?

   ____

   ____

5. Were you reminded of any mistakes that you've made in the past? Take a moment and ask the Lord to forgive you and give you the strength to walk in His ways moving forward.

   ____

   ____

Day 29

Proverbs 29

1 He who is often reproved, yet stiffens his neck, will suddenly be broken beyond healing.

2 When the righteous increase, the people rejoice, but when the wicked rule, the people groan.

3 He who loves wisdom makes his father glad, but a companion of prostitutes squanders his wealth.

4 By justice a king builds up the land, but he who exacts gifts[a] tears it down.

5 A man who flatters his neighbor spreads a net for his feet.

6 An evil man is ensnared in his transgression, but a righteous man sings and rejoices.

7 A righteous man knows the rights of the poor; a wicked man does not understand such knowledge.

8 Scoffers set a city aflame, but the wise turn away wrath.

9 If a wise man has an argument with a fool, the fool only rages and laughs, and there is no quiet.

10 Bloodthirsty men hate one who is blameless and seek the life of the upright.[b]

11 A fool gives full vent to his spirit, but a wise man quietly holds it back.

12 If a ruler listens to falsehood, all his officials will be wicked.

13 The poor man and the oppressor meet together; the Lord gives light to the eyes of both.

14 If a king faithfully judges the poor, his throne will be established forever.

15 The rod and reproof give wisdom, but a child left to himself brings shame to his mother.

16 When the wicked increase, transgression increases, but the righteous will look upon their downfall.

17 Discipline your son, and he will give you rest; he will give delight to your heart.

18 Where there is no prophetic vision the people cast off restraint,[c] but blessed is he who keeps the law.

19 By mere words a servant is not disciplined, for though he understands, he will not respond.

20 Do you see a man who is hasty in his words? There is more hope for a fool than for him.

21 Whoever pampers his servant from childhood will in the end find him his heir.[d]

22 A man of wrath stirs up strife, and one given to anger causes much transgression.

23 One's pride will bring him low, but he who is lowly in spirit will obtain honor.

24 The partner of a thief hates his own life; he hears the curse, but discloses nothing.

25 The fear of man lays a snare, but whoever trusts in the Lord is safe.

26 Many seek the face of a ruler, but it is from the Lord that a man gets justice.

27 An unjust man is an abomination to the righteous, but one whose way is straight is an abomination to the wicked.

---

a. Proverbs 29:4 Or *who taxes heavily* | b. Proverbs 29:10 Or *but the upright seek his soul* | c. Proverbs 29:18 Or *the people are discouraged* | d. Proverbs 29:21 The meaning of the Hebrew word rendered *his heir* is uncertain

Notes...

Reflection Questions...

As you read today's chapter in Proverbs

1. Did a verse or group of verses catch your attention? If so, why?

   a. How can you apply this wisdom in your life today/this week?

   b. Will you make the effort to commit this verse (or verses) to memory?

2. Did you see a recurring theme?

   a. If so, why is this theme important in our lives?

   b. How could applying this wisdom change your life and/or your relationships with others?

3. Did you find something you could praise God for? Take a moment to thank Him for a few blessings today.

4. Did you find a verse that you can incorporate in your time of prayer with God?

5. Were you reminded of any mistakes that you've made in the past? Take a moment and ask the Lord to forgive you and give you the strength to walk in His ways moving forward.

Day 30

Proverbs 30

The Words of Agur

1 The words of Agur son of Jakeh. The oracle.[a] The man declares, I am weary, O God; I am weary, O God, and worn out.[b]

2 Surely I am too stupid to be a man. I have not the understanding of a man.

3 I have not learned wisdom, nor have I knowledge of the Holy One.

4 Who has ascended to heaven and come down? Who has gathered the wind in his fists? Who has wrapped up the waters in a garment? Who has established all the ends of the earth? What is his name, and what is his son's name? Surely you know!

5 Every word of God proves true; he is a shield to those who take refuge in him.

6 Do not add to his words, lest he rebuke you and you be found a liar.

7 Two things I ask of you; deny them not to me before I die:

8 Remove far from me falsehood and lying; give me neither poverty nor riches; feed me with the food that is needful for me,

9 lest I be full and deny you and say, "Who is the Lord?" or lest I be poor and steal and profane the name of my God.

10 Do not slander a servant to his master, lest he curse you, and you be held guilty.

11 There are those[c] who curse their fathers and do not bless their mothers.

12 There are those who are clean in their own eyes but are not washed of their filth.

13 There are those—how lofty are their eyes, how high their eyelids lift!

14 There are those whose teeth are swords, whose fangs are knives, to devour the poor from off the earth, the needy from among mankind.

15 The leech has two daughters: Give and Give.[d] Three things are never satisfied; four never say, "Enough":

16 Sheol, the barren womb, the land never satisfied with water, and the fire that never says, "Enough."

17 The eye that mocks a father and scorns to obey a mother will be picked out by the ravens of the valley and eaten by the vultures.

18 Three things are too wonderful for me; four I do not understand:

19 the way of an eagle in the sky, the way of a serpent on a rock, the way of a ship on the high seas, and the way of a man with a virgin.

20 This is the way of an adulteress: she eats and wipes her mouth and says, "I have done no wrong."

21 Under three things the earth trembles; under four it cannot bear up:

22 a slave when he becomes king, and a fool when he is filled with food;

23 an unloved woman when she gets a husband, and a maidservant when she displaces her mistress.

24 Four things on earth are small, but they are exceedingly wise:

25 the ants are a people not strong, yet they provide their food in the summer;

26 the rock badgers are a people not mighty, yet they make their homes in the cliffs;

27 the locusts have no king, yet all of them march in rank;

28 the lizard you can take in your hands, yet it is in kings' palaces.

29 Three things are stately in their tread; four are stately in their stride:

30 the lion, which is mightiest among beasts and does not turn back before any;

31 the strutting rooster,[e] the he-goat, and a king whose army is with him.[f]

32 If you have been foolish, exalting yourself, or if you have been devising evil, put your hand on your mouth.

33 For pressing milk produces curds, pressing the nose produces blood, and pressing anger produces strife.

---

a. Proverbs 30:1 Or *Jakeh, the man of Massa* | b. Proverbs 30:1 Revocalization; Hebrew *The man declares to Ithiel, to Ithiel and Ucal* | c. Proverbs 30:11 Hebrew *There is a generation*; also verses 12, 13, 14 | d. Proverbs 30:15 Or *"Give, give," they cry* | e. Proverbs 30:31 Or *the magpie*, or *the greyhound*; Hebrew *girt-of-loins* | f. Proverbs 30:31 Or *against whom there is no rising up*

Notes...

Reflection Questions...

As you read today's chapter in Proverbs

1. Did a verse or group of verses catch your attention? If so, why?

   a. How can you apply this wisdom in your life today/this week?

   b. Will you make the effort to commit this verse (or verses) to memory?

2. Did you see a recurring theme?

   a. If so, why is this theme important in our lives?

   b. How could applying this wisdom change your life and/or your relationships with others?

3. Did you find something you could praise God for? Take a moment to thank Him for a few blessings today.

4. Did you find a verse that you can incorporate in your time of prayer with God?

5. Were you reminded of any mistakes that you've made in the past? Take a moment and ask the Lord to forgive you and give you the strength to walk in His ways moving forward.

Day 31

Proverbs 31

The Words of King Lemuel

1 The words of King Lemuel. An oracle that his mother taught him:

2 What are you doing, my son?[a] What are you doing, son of my womb? What are you doing, son of my vows?

3 Do not give your strength to women, your ways to those who destroy kings.

4 It is not for kings, O Lemuel, it is not for kings to drink wine, or for rulers to take strong drink,

5 lest they drink and forget what has been decreed and pervert the rights of all the afflicted.

6 Give strong drink to the one who is perishing, and wine to those in bitter distress;[b]

7 let them drink and forget their poverty and remember their misery no more.

8 Open your mouth for the mute, for the rights of all who are destitute.[c]

9 Open your mouth, judge righteously, defend the rights of the poor and needy.

The Woman Who Fears the Lord

10 [d] An excellent wife who can find? She is far more precious than jewels.

11 The heart of her husband trusts in her, and he will have no lack of gain.

12 She does him good, and not harm, all the days of her life.

13 She seeks wool and flax, and works with willing hands.

14 She is like the ships of the merchant; she brings her food from afar.

15 She rises while it is yet night and provides food for her household and portions for her maidens.

16 She considers a field and buys it; with the fruit of her hands she plants a vineyard.

17 She dresses herself[e] with strength and makes her arms strong.

18 She perceives that her merchandise is profitable. Her lamp does not go out at night.

19 She puts her hands to the distaff, and her hands hold the spindle.

20 She opens her hand to the poor and reaches out her hands to the needy.

21 She is not afraid of snow for her household, for all her household are clothed in scarlet.[f]

22 She makes bed coverings for herself; her clothing is fine linen and purple.

23 Her husband is known in the gates when he sits among the elders of the land.

24 She makes linen garments and sells them; she delivers sashes to the merchant.

25 Strength and dignity are her clothing, and she laughs at the time to come.

26 She opens her mouth with wisdom, and the teaching of kindness is on her tongue.

27 She looks well to the ways of her household and does not eat the bread of idleness.

28 Her children rise up and call her blessed; her husband also, and he praises her:

29 "Many women have done excellently, but you surpass them all."

30 Charm is deceitful, and beauty is vain, but a woman who fears the Lord is to be praised.

31 Give her of the fruit of her hands, and let her works praise her in the gates.

---

a. Proverbs 31:2 Hebrew *What, my son?* | b. Proverbs 31:6 Hebrew *those bitter in soul* | c. Proverbs 31:8 Hebrew *are sons of passing away* | d. Proverbs 31:10 Verses 10–31 are an acrostic poem, each verse beginning with the successive letters of the Hebrew alphabet | e. Proverbs 31:17 Hebrew *She girds her loins* | f. Proverbs 31:21 Or *in double thickness*

Notes...

Reflection Questions...

As you read today's chapter in Proverbs

1. Did a verse or group of verses catch your attention? If so, why?

   a. How can you apply this wisdom in your life today/this week?

   b. Will you make the effort to commit this verse (or verses) to memory?

2. Did you see a recurring theme?

   a. If so, why is this theme important in our lives?

   b. How could applying this wisdom change your life and/or your relationships with others?

3. Did you find something you could praise God for? Take a moment to thank Him for a few blessings today.

4. Did you find a verse that you can incorporate in your time of prayer with God?

5. Were you reminded of any mistakes that you've made in the past? Take a moment and ask the Lord to forgive you and give you the strength to walk in His ways moving forward.

Summary Page

I sincerely hope the past thirty-one days have been a time of learning and growth for you. The Bible says in Romans 12:2 that we are to be transformed by the renewal of our minds, and there is no greater tool to transform you than the truth found in God's word!

It is my prayer that finishing this book will not be a stopping point for you or a checkbox that you will mark as completed. My desire is that this is just the beginning of a lifelong journey through the book of Proverbs and walking in Wisdom. May you continue to grow in discernment, understanding, and the love of Christ Jesus our great Counselor and King. The wisdom of God has no end, and it is a worthy pursuit to continually seek and strive after the heart and mind of God every day of your life!

Receive His words . . .
Treasure His commandments within you . . .
Make your ear attentive to wisdom . . .
Incline your heart to understanding . . .
Call out for insight . . .
Raise your voice for understanding . . .
Seek it like silver and search for it as hidden treasures . . .
a rendering of Proverbs 2:1–4

"*. . . then you will understand the fear of the LORD and find the knowledge of God. For the LORD gives wisdom; from his mouth come knowledge and understanding; he stores up sound wisdom for the upright; he is a shield to those who walk in integrity, guarding the paths of justice and watching over the way of his saints. Then you will understand righteousness and justice and equity, every good path; for wisdom will come into your heart, and knowledge will be pleasant to your soul; discretion will watch over you, understanding will guard you...*"
Proverbs 2:5–11

About the Author

Growing up on a dirt road in a small town in southwest Missouri gave Trog a love for nature and God's creation at a young age. After graduating high school, he attended Campbell University in North Carolina where he earned his bachelor's degree and master's degree in Business Administration. After finishing his degrees, Trog came to Texas for a business opportunity, but the Lord had different plans. Over the past decade, he has served in multiple ministry endeavors, such as being a Cares Team with Apartment Life Ministries, helping plant a church in Frisco, and being a Discipleship Minister with Christ Church Plano. He now serves as an Urban Gardener and Spiritual/Community Developer in south Dallas where he invests his time in God's creation, growing food for those in need, and making disciples.

Trog is married to a beautiful woman named Mendi and has three children, Sevyn, Rok, and Truth. If you get to spend time with him, you will often hear him talking about seeking first the Kingdom, losing your life in order to save it, and the importance of discipleship. He is passionate about sharing his faith in Christ, helping the poor, and making disciples.

His favorite verses: Psalm 1:1–3 / Matthew 6:33
His blog: www.KingdomMotivated.com
His voice for the poor: www.Project2540.com

Please visit Trog's website www.AWalkToWisdom.com to find out more about him and other ministries that he loves to support. Or send him an e-mail at trogtrogdon@gmail.com.

About Supported Ministries

100 percent of the profits from the sales of this book will go to Kingdom causes. Bonton Farm Works and H.I.S. Bridgebuilders benevolence fund have been chosen as the first two recipients of the funds generated from this resource.

About Bonton Farm-Works

Bonton Farm-Works is an urban discipleship and farming initiative designed to restore health (both physically and spiritually) to a poverty stricken community in south Dallas. Bonton is a neighborhood located in the middle of a "food desert" where people are sick and even dying from the lack of healthy, affordable food. The work and prayer of this ministry is designed to bring hope and restoration to this wonderful community for the glory of God and the advancement of His Kingdom.

About H.I.S. Bridgebuilders

H.I.S. Bridgebuilders is a movement of God uniting Christians across cities to restore urban communities through education, health, economic development, and spiritual development. The benevolence ministry of H.I.S. Bridgebuilders contributes to housing costs, utility bills, medical bills, food, clothing concerns, and more for people in times of need.